Testim...
Bipola...

Ray Sturt reports a remarkable recove... through a painful experience, and their ... others who suffer from this condition. ... ...d hope to

—**Charles C. Todd, Jr.,** EdD
Retired teacher and school administrator

My wife, Belle, and I have watched for over forty years with wonder and amazement at the incredible victories we have seen accomplished in both Linda and Ray's lives.

—**Edwin Jaeger**
Brother-in-law and former missionary to Iran

In my conversations with Ray Sturt, I have found him to be honest, imaginative, and dedicated. Though I have not yet read his completed manuscript, I am confident that his readers will find his words stimulating and helpful in developing a sensitivity for those who wrestle with this difficult manifestation that causes such turmoil and unrest in their lives.

—**Rev. Robert H. Armstrong**
Retired Episcopal priest

Ray and Linda Sturt have coauthored an important book on an underappreciated problem that affects all too many people. Their true, insightful story fills a crucial gap and is deeply inspiring.

—**John B. Rosenman,** PhD
Professor of English, Norfolk State University

My wife, Poppy, and I have known Ray and Linda Sturt for over fourteen years. These trustworthy and very dependable friends have shown almost-unbelievable dedication to one another and hurting family and friends around them and have persevered through all the hurts and pains that life has thrown at them. Indeed they are more than conquerors!

—**Rev. Larry C. Miles**

Ray and Linda have a story to tell. I've known Ray and Linda for many years and have seen this story firsthand. I can truly attest from their witness that Christ offers profound healing and hope for those wrestling with bipolar disorder. Ray and Linda embody this healing and hope.

—**Thomas Price**
PhD, Oxford University

I have known Ray Sturt for many years. He has done an amazing job handling the problem of bipolar disease. Good luck to you!

—**Jerome Skaggs**, MD

The Sturts have been my friends for many years. They are wonderful Christian people who seek to honor God and spread His truth. I am privileged to know them and to be part of their lives. They have always encouraged me and my family and have prayed for us and loved us regardless of our situation or circumstances. They are faithful believers, compassionate and caring people who have trusted God even when their lives have been touched by illness and tragedy.

—**Grace Cheely**
BS, Bob Jones University, home economics & science
Former teacher, Portsmouth Christian Schools

I have known Ray and Linda Sturt for the last eight years as friends and fellow tennis enthusiasts. Their passion and persistence in communicating their life experiences is admirable. I wish them both much success in their endeavors to inform and encourage others through their book.

—**Rose H. Baldwin**, CPA

BIPOLAR VICTORY

BIPOLAR VICTORY

RAY AND LINDA STURT
WITH ROBIN STANLEY

WinePressPublishing
Great Books, Defined.

© 2013 by Ray and Linda Sturt with Robin Stanley. All rights reserved.

WinePress Publishing (PO Box 428, Enumclaw, WA 98022) functions only as book publisher. As such, the ultimate design, content, editorial accuracy, and views expressed or implied in this work are those of the author.

No part of this publication may be reproduced, stored in a retrieval system, or transmitted in any way by any means—electronic, mechanical, photocopy, recording, or otherwise—without the prior permission of the copyright holder, except as provided by USA copyright law.

To protect friends and family from the potential grief and embarrassment of making difficult personal circumstances public, the authors deliberately used fictitious names for people other than those in their immediate family.

Visit www.bipolarvictory.com.

Unless otherwise noted, all Scriptures are taken from the *Holy Bible, New International Version®, NIV®*. Copyright © 1973, 1978, 1984 by Biblica, Inc.™ Used by permission of Zondervan. All rights reserved worldwide. www.zondervan.com

Scripture references marked NKJV are taken from the *New King James Version®*. Copyright © 1982 by Thomas Nelson, Inc. Used by permission. All rights reserved.

Scripture references marked KJV are taken from the *King James Version* of the Bible.

ISBN 13: 978-1-60615-014-6
ISBN 10: 1-60615-014-6
Library of Congress Catalog Card Number: 2009928161

The authors intend for the testimonials within this book to encourage and inspire, not to propose treatment for any illness or provide any sort of medical advice. They should not be presumed a substitute for professional medical or psychiatric care but are for informational purposes only. This book is not intended to take the place of professional medical or psychiatric advice, diagnosis, or treatment. Always seek the advice of your physician or other qualified health-care provider with any questions you may have regarding a medical or psychiatric condition. Never disregard professional medical or psychiatric advice or delay in seeking it because of something you have read. The authors shall have neither liability nor responsibility to any individual or entity with respect to any loss, damage, or injury caused or alleged to be caused directly or indirectly by the information presented in this book.

I dedicate this book to the glory and praise of God,
for His purposes fulfilled in my life.
To my loving, devoted family—my wife, Linda,
and my sons, Scott and Adam—
you remained by my side throughout my struggle
with bipolar disorder.
Because you refused to let go, we can celebrate victory together.
I'm grateful.

CONTENTS

Acknowledgments xiii

1. An Elusive Opponent. 1
2. Snares Exposed. 5
3. An Emerging Alliance 21
4. An Established Home Front. 39
5. Encroachment 53
6. Rules of Engagement 75
7. Behind Enemy Lines 85
8. Engulfed. 99
9. Surrender Explored 111
10. Unexpected Lifeline 119
11. A Lifesaving Encounter 127
12. Suffering Endured 139
13. Everlasting Victory. 151

Epilogue. 157

Notes 171

ACKNOWLEDGMENTS

It has been a privilege and a most enlightening and enjoyable experience to work with Robin Stanley. Thank you, Robin, for your diligent patience with us along this journey and for keeping us in line with the requirements necessary to professionally publish our story. Because you listened with great compassion and insight, we have together reached the summit of our pursuit. Well done!

Special thanks to Dr. Charles Todd, the tennis guru who inspired us to write and publish this book.

CHAPTER 1

AN ELUSIVE OPPONENT

I'm a tired man. Sometimes I think I'm the tiredest man on earth.
—Abraham Lincoln

"I WANT OUT!" The groan that had been festering for years finally erupted, spewing its poison all over the woman I adored.

Linda stood speechless at the foot of our bed. Her knees buckled under the weight of my hurtful words. She didn't deserve this heartache.

Out of control, spiraling toward the bottomless pit from which I could never climb out, I ran. Grabbing my bike from the shed, I pedaled as fast as I could down our county road. Tears mixed with sweat flew from my face in the heat of that July afternoon. The wind took my breath away, swallowing my desperate cries for everything to come to an end. But nothing could stop the loop that played over and over in my mind, like a soundtrack for every move: *I must be the most horrible person in the world.*

A mile and a half later, I swung onto the drive that led to Bermuda Memorial Park. The peace and quiet of this cemetery usually helped me get a grip when the battles in my life became too much to handle. Not today. Today the contrast only made the turmoil seem bigger and my mind race faster. So troubled. So distressed.

Shade from the familiar trees did little to comfort my broken spirit. I straddled the crossbar of my bike and scanned the canopy overhead. Anger surged. I tried to silence its threat by deliberately choosing a branch strong enough to hold my body weight.

Twelve years. Twelve long years of suicidal thoughts and homicidal intentions. Twelve years filled with short glimpses of elation followed by long, dark periods of depression, most lasting for days. Disturbing voices in my head chased and taunted me, an endless torment.

The devastation consumed my life. Bipolar illness laid siege to every territory it touched: my job, my marriage, my health, my family, even my faith.

On one November night, swirling emotions took me closer to the edge of despair than I'd ever been. *End it!* the inner voices whispered. *End it all. Why not? Can you really call this a life?*

"Enough!" I shouted back. "I've had enough!" The words cut through the chill and echoed down my spine. Darkness covered me. The end of my rope hung very near. *How can I live the rest of my life in this wretched condition?* Desperation turned into heaving sobs as I stood without clothing and without courage in the middle of our hot tub. "Oh, GOD! Please, have your way with me!"

Millions of people all over the world stand in this desperate darkness, suffering from the same debilitating symptoms. The Depression and Bipolar Support Alliance reports that bipolar disorder affects six million adults in America alone, and only a fraction of those affected receive treatment.[1] Sometimes it starts in the early years of childhood, but it comes upon most people somewhere around twenty-five years of age. Why had it happened to me at forty-three?

Most specialists prefer to call bipolar illness by its more-common name, manic depression. But simplifying the name doesn't change its unforgiving,

AN ELUSIVE OPPONENT

erratic nature. The mania makes you feel like you could fly. Energy levels soar and everybody loves you. You're the life of the party—until the depression comes back around. And believe me, when it comes, as it always will, it hits hard. No wonder the illness drives so many sufferers to the brink of suicide, with one in five actually taking his own life.

While I am one of the four in five who did not complete a suicide attempt, I often wished I had. Psychiatrists tried to help, but none of their powerful prescriptions could even begin to touch the dark, unstable places inside me. I tried lithium carbonate, Depakote, Geodon, Trileptal—all with no success. I was locked in a battle with an elusive opponent, against which I felt powerless, stripped down, laid bare, defeated.

I was tired. Tired of the fight. Tired of being out of control. Tired of the toll this siege was taking on my family.

My only out? Surrender. Let it have my life so everyone else could get on with living theirs.

Why not? I only brought them grief—embarrassment, ugliness, and grief. On top of the uncontrolled behavior, they had to deal with my pressured speech. I talked nonstop, most of the time with no idea what I said. I ranted about the government and my neighbors and yelled at innocent telemarketers. When my tongue took over, I could do nothing to make it stop. I spoke terrible lies about my beloved wife and even cussed at my sons. Imagine having to watch as your father tears apart your family. And I know I broke my wife's heart.

They all deserved so much more than me.

But here's the kicker: they wouldn't let me go. Unbelievable. Somehow, my family found a way to live with me because they didn't want to live without me. No matter how many times I threatened my wife's life or begged her for a divorce, she steadfastly refused to leave. Linda became my advocate, dedicated and resolute. Not just *toward* me but *for* me, daily crying out to the Lord for a miracle. And I mean to tell you, a miracle was about the only chance we had left.

If you're struggling to gain ground in a battle against bipolar disorder or if you know someone who is, you know the desperation. And you know too well the havoc the disease wreaks on everything and everyone it touches. But you also need to know you're not alone.

BIPOLAR VICTORY

Most of the psychiatrists I've spoken with agree that the bipolar population is growing. It's reaching into more and more communities, tearing more and more families apart, without prejudice of age, gender, or race.

That's why Linda and I decided to tell our story.

Some call us courageous to pull back the curtain on the details of our lives. But courage isn't found in the telling, it's discovered in the living.

CHAPTER 2

SNARES EXPOSED

I have come to realize more and more that the greatest disease and the greatest suffering is to be unwanted, unloved, uncared for, to be shunned by everybody, to be just nobody to no one.
—Mother Theresa of Calcutta

Born in Petersburg, Virginia, on April 23, 1947, I spent my growing-up years playing among the dug-out mounds of some of the most famous battlegrounds in American history. The second brother in a band of three, I followed my oldest sibling everywhere. We excavated arrowheads, old bullets, belt buckles, and other extraordinary Civil War relics. Union General Ulysses S. Grant and Confederate General Robert E. Lee spent their days roaming the woods in our area, perhaps on the very trails where we road our bicycles.

The innocence of our youth kept us unaware of the significance of our discoveries or even the importance of our stomping grounds. I look back now and see much of my life mimicking the battles waged just beyond our backyard, some eighty-two years before I took my first breath.

Like the labored step of a young soldier trudging through his first mission, my first breaths did not come easy. Racked with convulsions and a high fever, my body denied its entry into the world. Sure that I wouldn't make it, my parents wondered whether they would need to dig a grave before they ever got to finish the nursery. But something, or Somebody, saw fit to keep me on this earth. For some unknown reason, the convulsions went away as quickly as they came, and I lived to experience more of life. Life, with all its twists and turns, its joys and its sorrows, its dangers and … its snares.

I learned early on that snares sneak up on you as if from nowhere. They can trip you up and keep you down, and no amount of kicking or screaming will get you out. Not even when people you love are within shouting distance.

Every year our family welcomed spring with the chug of an old Penn Craft rototiller. I can still hear the grind of its blades digging into the hard earth. It brings to mind a picture of my dad, his arms stretched out, the machine giving in to his strength. Dad spent a lot of time outdoors, especially during gardening season. He grew vegetables like nobody's business.

One spring afternoon, my father took my older brother and me out to watch him dig. "Stand there," he said. "And try to keep yourselves outta my way. If you know what's right, you'll keep a close eye on what I'm doing. You'll need to know how to work the ground when you get a little bigger."

I was two. And my brother was only nearing four. To hear my brother tell the story, Dad got himself all tied up in his strong man routine, punching big holes in the ground with his new posthole digger, and he forgot all about us. Which, normally, would have been a good thing for two small boys running free in the yard on a sunny day. But on that day, it nearly cost me my life. Remember those snares? Well, one snuck up on me, and my dad dug it!

Dad remembered that he turned to pitch the digger back down into the hole to make it deeper when he noticed my brother jumping up and down, frantic. "I could barely hear him," Dad said. "But I knew something wasn't right. He kept hollering, 'Bubba! Bubba!' So I dropped the digger, and I looked over the edge of the hole. Guess who was at the bottom?"

Dad asked Mom that question every time he told the story. Like she would be one to forget. "There was your boy, Ray, all blue in the face," he said, answering his own question with a chuckle. "He done knocked the wind right outta himself."

Dad grabbed my feet that day and freed me from the dark hole. But there would be days to come when I would wish he hadn't.

Life in the Sturt household seemed all-American to most—even to us. Mom tried her best to make it so. On days when we needed relief, she flicked the television switch and spilled hours of happiness into the house. Larry, Moe, and Curly's antics more than delighted us every day after school. Nothing could beat the swashbuckling, pipe-swinging guffaws of *The Three Stooges*. Their slapstick humor always brought out the best of our belly laughs. And when the Sturt boys were laughing, all seemed right in the world.

I remember one episode where a radio-show host mistook Curly for an opera singer. The image of Curly with a fruit basket on his head, imitating the performance of a classically trained soprano, still makes me chuckle. The truth came to light when an irritated violinist pulled the plug on the phonograph while Curly sang, accompanied by Larry and Moe, at the host's swanky party. The trio of imposters hid under the piano to escape the outcry of the angry crowd, though not for long. Three grown men do not FIT under a piano!

As a kid, I didn't enjoy drawing attention to myself. So like the Three Stooges, I got good at hiding. Behind humor, behind obedience, behind the shed when my dad wanted me to do something I didn't want to do. Sometimes I hid in my silence, right out in the open.

When I was in the third grade, Dad stopped by my classroom one afternoon. "Mrs. Smith, it's nice to see you again," he said, reaching out to shake her hand. "I'm here to pick up my son. We have an appointment across town."

"Why, thank you, Mr. Sturt," replied Mrs. Smith. She always wore a polite smile. "It's good to see you too. But we haven't seen Ray all day."

Without missing a beat, my father stepped toward my desk. Gesturing, he directed me to join him. "Son, come on up here and introduce yourself to your teacher."

Compliant and unwilling to cross my dad, I gave up hiding in my silence and did as I was told. The whole way to the front of the room, I wished real hard I was dreaming. A shy boy had a bad enough time among the mean kids without being called out and made a fool of … by his own dad. If I could have ducked out the door without saying a word, I would have. But Dad insisted. Why must he always insist?

I reached the teacher's desk and extended my right hand. "How do you do, Mrs. Smith? My name is Ray. Ray Sturt, ma'am." The class erupted in laughter. I felt heat rise up from my toes and set my skin ablaze. It may have been my dad's intent to call out the teacher in his charismatic way. But I'm the one who suffered the consequences of his intrusion that day.

No nine-year-old could have held back any better than I did. Once I climbed into the front seat of my dad's Ford pickup, I turned my face toward the window. Even awkward silence makes for a suitable hiding place.

Silence became, for me, a way to manage the awkwardness of our family interactions. I solved many problems as a kid while sitting on top of our backyard picnic table. Surrounded by gardens, trees, and pastures, I enjoyed a perfect view from my perch. I could see Mom caring for the chickens and milking the cow. I watched squirrels and rabbits scurrying about. I loved to lie back and lose myself in the clouds as I mused on the meaning of life. Why was I here? Was my time on earth only to be endured?

I may have been young, but my mind sought answers to questions that couldn't possibly be asked, let alone answered. Dad sure didn't have the time or patience to hear the depth of my childish inquiries. He believed in hard work that yielded great gain. Nothing more, and certainly nothing less.

Required to live by strictly imposed boundaries and expectations, I buried my questions and learned what I needed to do in order to please my dad. At a young age, I began mowing the lawn with our cub tractor, gathering empty pop bottles from the side of the road so my brothers and I could buy sodas at the store, selling extra garden vegetables from bags on my bike, and scrubbing our four-by-four-foot custom-built shower stall every week. One summer, Dad decided to add another room onto the house. Guess who dug and hauled dirt to prepare the foundation? Yes, and Dad was pleased.

These experiences with my dad, while giving me more good hiding places, laid a solid foundation for later years when I would be responsible to provide for a family. In short order, I developed a strong work ethic and began to understand that nothing is free. Everything that's worth anything costs you something. And some things … well, they can cost you nearly everything.

My father decided to supplement his income as a soil-conservation agent for Prince George County by developing a mobile home park. Over the course of several weeks, he sold the milk cow and mowed down the pasture. Then he and Mom worked to set twelve trailers on the acreage just beyond the vegetable garden and proudly put up a sign next to the road advertising Hilltop Trailer Park. Dad continued to work for the county, and Mom managed nearly everything to do with the business growing in our backyard. She parked new trailers, found the tenants, collected the rent, dealt with issues and complaints, and cleaned the trailers when the tenants moved out. Day and night the demands increased, especially for Mom. Any time was business time at the Sturt's. We couldn't even count on meals together without the doorbell ringing.

When the next thirty trailers went in all the way up the hill in the back, the calls became relentless. The pressure to perform became intense. Dad's rarely pleasant demeanor turned completely sour, and Mom could do very little to please him. Our home became a very unhappy place to raise three boys. Bickering became the backdrop for everyday events—waking up, eating lunch, watching television, and even going to bed.

One evening as my brothers and I flipped channels to find a nice distraction from the shouting spilling over from Mom's room, the piercing sound of gunfire jarred the night air.

One round.

My older brother hit the off button on the television, and we stared at each other in silence. A silence not right for hiding, though I never wished so hard to be invisible.

After what seemed like hours—though it was probably only minutes, maybe even seconds—my dad appeared in the doorway. His stern voice broke the glaring silence but offered little comfort and no explanation.

"Boys, it's time to go to bed."

I didn't want to go to bed. I wanted an explanation. I wanted to run and hide.

What would John Wayne do? I wondered. He was, after all, my childhood hero. Then I remembered a line he delivered as Ringo Kid in the movie *Stagecoach*. "There are some things a man just can't run away from."

John Wayne was no longer my hero.

How could I respond in obedience to a father who failed to see that his sons were mortified? Worse yet, what if he saw and chose to do nothing? And where was Mom? Did Dad not know that we would want to know? These questions should not be unanswerable, let alone unutterable.

"Yes, sir," we responded in unison.

Still shuddering from the effects of an event that would hold our family captive for years, we walked past a man who required our respect.

I wanted him to earn it.

Evidently, so did Mom. She had pulled a Smith & Weston on him. The bullet lodged in the hardwood floor. The same pistol they purchased to help protect our family contributed to tearing our family apart.

Mom told us later she hadn't intended to pull the trigger.

We never mentioned the incident again. But painful shouts continued long after that night. Daily quarrels. Relentless accusations. Constant profanities.

Peace did not reside at the Sturt house. We looked for it elsewhere. And what we could not find, we faked.

Someone asked me recently if I attended church as a kid. I did. Every week. It meant extra work for Dad on Saturdays, including filling up the car with gas. The blue laws of those days required businesses to close on Sundays. In spite of the hassle, Dad always made sure we went to church as a family. I don't know whether it was part of the looking for peace or the faking. Whatever the case, it didn't yield much. I grew up with little knowledge of the Bible and no relationship with God.

Every week after church, we came home for a delicious home-cooked dinner. My brothers and I rushed to get out of our Sunday clothes so we could play outside with Freto while Mom got dinner ready. Freto lived in a penthouse of doghouses that we built with our very own hands. Constructed up off the ground, it had a special fenced-in area where he loved to hang out in the sun. But Freto also loved his freedom. Running free with us up and down the road made Freto a very happy beagle.

In our backyard, just off the porch, hung a large iron dinner bell. When we heard Mom clanging on that bell, we knew it was time to hurry home for our favorite meal of the week—country-fried chicken, potatoes, and green beans from our garden.

After dinner, we often piled into the car and drove to the old farm in McKinney where Dad was raised. As far as family time went, this was as good as it got. We loved the old home place, as it was affectionately known. The whole family gathered for great fun. Aunts, uncles, and cousins ran through the fields and played rousing games of baseball. We drank cool, clear water straight from the spring at the side of the house.

These were sweet, lifesaving days I would look back on and even try to imitate as life went by. Sprinkled in with *The Three Stooges, Gunsmoke,* John Wayne, and my mom, they made the demands of my childhood a little more bearable.

Mom understood the demands. She could do little to make them go away, but she did what she could to provide moments of relief. Along with the television shows, Mom gave us music. It became something we all looked forward to, a source of comfort, something we all shared and everyone needed.

Saturday evenings were reserved for *The Lawrence Welk Show*. But every weekday morning, Mom turned on the TV so we could start our day in a peaceful way—with Liberace! His talent for playing the piano fascinated me. Watching his fingers fly over the keys lifted my spirits and made me believe happiness might be possible, somewhere. Somehow. Sometime. I wondered if I crossed my fingers and wished real hard whether happiness might become something normal instead of something we hoped for. I didn't know then that this kind of happiness doesn't really fill a person up the way a person needs to be filled.

With Mom managing the backyard business and Dad always working, we all had holes that needed filling. Big holes. Music covered them for a time, but it could not fill them. It allowed us a temporary escape from the madness of our lives. I read once that music is supposed to be some sort of universal language. I reckon that for us it was. Mom used it as a way to tell us she loved us. She was too worn out to use a language all her own.

My frustrations built up while I hid in silence, but I soon learned a language of my own for letting them out. Football! Or basketball! Or high jumping! Right out in the yard. When I hit and ran and tossed and leaped, my body felt strong. My soul felt free. I also enjoyed archery and golf. As it turned out, sports became a good outlet for me. I possessed a God-given athleticism. Since Mom and Dad needed us to be available to work at the house or in the trailer park, I didn't compete at school. I'm sure I could have. Instead, I spent every minute I could get outside engaged in some sort of physical activity. I had found a great hiding place. A way to be the strong, expressive person I was designed to be. Who cared if anyone noticed?

Few things my brothers and I did as kids ever gained much attention from my parents, especially not the positive kind. Their words of praise were sparse; their words of love even sparser. Not only toward us, but also toward each other. Whether they were ignorant of childrearing or simply lacked the ability to express something they had not experienced, the results crippled us, all of us. At times, the incapacitation became a threat to our very lives.

One summer afternoon, while shooting baskets in the backyard, I became aware of an intense pain in my side. As I had learned to do over the course of my thirteen years, I played through the pain. After another twenty jumpers, rotating corner to corner, I hit a wall. The searing heat shot through me like the tail of a rocket, and I crumbled.

I could see my little brother standing over me. His young voice echoed in slow motion, "Mooommmyyy! Help Ray!" I reached out for him to help me up, but he wasn't strong enough. I couldn't move. Everything started spinning and suddenly went black.

I woke up in the backseat of my dad's Ford Fairlane.

"Why does that boy always get himself into these situations? He falls into holes and out of trees. It's always somethin'. What did he do this time? Trip over his shoelace? Like I have all the time in the world to deal with this."

Dad's voice sounded a little warbled, but I couldn't mistake the tone. Why must everything always be about him? His inconvenience? His embarrassment? His waste of time? The pain was unbearable. I wished I hadn't woken up.

"Joe, don't be so hard on Ray. Can't you see that—"

A sudden scream interrupted the quiet of my mom's voice. I didn't recognize it at the time, but that scream came from me. Something was wrong. Terribly wrong.

The doctor came into the examination room just as soon as they wheeled me in. After asking a few questions that my mom tried to answer, he put his hand on my abdomen.

"Ye-ow!" My knee shot up and about hit him square on the nose.

Several pokes and a couple of needles later, the doc announced that I needed immediate surgery. Acute appendicitis.

When I heard the word *surgery*, I would have run if I could. I was normally a pretty brave kid. But in that moment, I didn't feel brave at all.

My dad took the news as poorly as I did, though for a different reason. When Dad heard the word *surgery*, he shook his head in disagreement and put on his hat. "Come on, son, let's go."

I couldn't believe my ears.

The doctor intervened and invited my parents to step into the hall with him. I could hear them arguing, first my mom and then my dad.

"Absolutely not, Alice. We're going home."

Why did my parents always have to argue? Why did my dad always insist that he get his way?

Then something happened that confounds me to this day. Mom stood up to him. "Joe, if you're not going to sign those release papers, I will. Ray's in trouble."

"Ray's in trouble." Those words hung in my mind as I drifted off to sleep.

My appendix came out. The surgery went well, and within a couple of days, the doctor sent me home to mend. The pain of the incision in my side seemed a small exchange for the amount of pain I had been in.

The surgical wound healed quickly. The wound inflicted by hearing my parents fight over whether I needed surgery did not. It became a pain that, mixed with all the other hurts piled up inside, lingered with me well into my adult years.

All this heartache sent me further into isolation from my family and forced me into adulthood sooner than some might expect. Under the control of my father, I had no choice. I knew I needed to make my own way, so I went looking for a job. A real job. And at sixteen, I landed one!

The same school district that told my mom I would never amount to much hired me to drive a sixty-six-passenger school bus. Me! Ray Sturt! I had two routes every single school day. In the early mornings,

SNARES EXPOSED

I made rounds to pick up the elementary school kids. Then after dropping them off, I went back out to pick up the high school kids.

I learned a lot about myself from that job. It gave me confidence to be Ray. I was glad to be working. Sometimes I forgot that it started out as a way to escape the Sturt household. And though my dad complained because I wasn't available to do as many chores at home, I think he may actually have been proud of me. He never did say so, but I overheard him talking to Mr. Deadmon down at the barbershop one day. "My boy Ray, he's driving one of our district school buses now," he said. "What do you think about that?"

Home remained a stressful place. But on the bus I had respite from being "pained in body and troubled in mind." That respite is what Thomas Jefferson called happiness. I would have to agree. In spite of needing occasional discipline, the kids brought with them a sense of delight I hadn't often experienced. My time with them made the rest of life a little more bearable. I suppose maybe some of their happiness rubbed off on me enough that I carried it throughout the day. They made me feel appreciated and rewarded me with presents during the Christmas season. I received pencils of every color, candy of every flavor, and enough pairs of gloves to last me a lifetime of winters.

Several hard winters passed, helped along by the refuge of my work, and I found myself ready to graduate from Prince George High School. Not with honors but with the distinct privilege of never missing a day of school due to illness. How many kids can say that? In my whole school career, I missed one day, the day of Grandma Sturt's funeral when I was in the sixth grade.

In spite of hating school because I had such a hard time reading, I had always preferred being at school rather than at home. So this accomplishment didn't seem to me to be a big deal. But for my dad it was, especially when the principal failed to acknowledge my perfect attendance at the graduation ceremony.

I didn't mind. I had become accustomed to being unnoticed. But it bothered Dad so much, he called the school to draw attention to their error. Thankfully, he didn't take me by the hand, march me into the office, and make me introduce myself to the principal. I don't think I could have endured reliving that third-grade embarrassment. But he did insist that something be done. Later in the month, I received my due embarrassment—an apology in the mail along with a very nice award that my dad promptly framed and posted on the wall.

It stated for all the world to see that Ray Sturt received an award for perfect attendance. My dad looked at it and beamed. It was his award, really, showing that his insistence paid off. It proved that he won—again. Yes, it was all about him. His pride. His shame at my being overlooked for my one claim to fame. I wondered how he would feel to know that I went to school every day to avoid staying at home with him. Digging his holes. Doing his chores. Mowing his lawn. Turning out his lights.

Some days I wished I had the courage to really turn out his lights.

After graduation, I redirected all the angst inside and took a job with the Virginia State Highway Department. We worked outdoors, patching the state roads with hot tar and gravel. I got really good at slinging that mess around. I liked to work hard. It kept my mind occupied and my body occupied, free from pain and distractions. I guess I found happiness once more outside our home. When I could work with my hands, I felt useful. It gave me a purpose for being that I couldn't satisfy in any other way.

I didn't fit in well with some of the roughneck guys who worked for the state. But I did make easy friends with an African-American fellow. We worked side by side and enjoyed each other's companionship. There's a lot to be gained when one finds acceptance from the point of view of another human being.

What we encountered, though, turned my stomach. Outright prejudice. We would be so thirsty our lips would seem to be cracking on the spot, but not a soul would give us a drink. Not even from an outside water hose. Now, what do you think about that? But we were a good pair, Bo and I. We shared well in the pain of rejection. That made us good buddies. We watched after one another. I wondered what would make a person so afraid of another person, just because of the color of his skin. Later in life, I would know that same kind of fear a little more personally than I did at the time.

SNARES EXPOSED

Fear can make people do strange things.

When I left that job to pursue an interest in work involving more precision, Bo and I parted ways. But I never forgot the man who seemed to be the spitting image of me, at least on the inside where character counts. Our paths would cross again someday; I knew it.

After meddling some in electronics, tearing out old wires and putting in new, I was hired to help the machinists at the E. E. Titus Foundry. I liked the work so much that within a few months I moved to Newport News and started training as an apprentice machinist at the Newport News Shipbuilding and Dry Dock Company. I don't think my dad noticed. But I had come not to care. I was making my way, and nothing he said or did would challenge the pride I held inside for the first time in my life.

One might say my giftedness in survival techniques came directly from my father. Because of our coexistence, I learned how to see a challenge and maneuver around it. Even when the battlegrounds shifted—from the mounds in our backyard to the winding state roads of Virginia and then to the steamy jungles of Vietnam—I could hold my own.

During this time the Vietnam War raged overseas, as well as in the minds of young men across our country. Not long after starting school, I found out my name would be coming up on the draft list as the government called many from our region into service. With a combat skill I learned from being in the war zone with my father, I ducked into a hiding place and quietly outmaneuvered the draft by joining the United States Army Reserves in April 1966. Once in the reserves, I could not be drafted into active duty for Vietnam when my name came up; I would already be fulfilling my civic responsibilities. Not that I was a coward. I was not. But I learned from my dad to control the things I could control before other people could step in to control me.

This attempt to choose my level of military involvement proved successful when, a year later, I reported for full-time duty at Fort Dix, New Jersey. Boot camp. Not a place for the weak to hide but a safe place for the strong to thrive. They put an M-16 rifle in my hands and challenged me until I became proficient. The training I received from my dad when he took me hunting turned out to be invaluable. The precision I learned in the woods from shooting squirrels with a double-barreled shotgun catapulted me quickly to expert sharpshooter status. I wondered whether people, particularly my dad, might notice me now. Me. Ray Sturt. Expert sharpshooter.

With this achievement, I qualified for a weekend pass. So I went home. I took a bus as far as Petersburg and walked the remaining six miles to my house. I must have been a sight, trudging along those dark country roads in my uniform and clunky combat boots.

Finally arriving in the quiet hours before dawn, I climbed into the backseat of my dad's now-aging Fairlane. Immediately my mind flashed back to the day I awoke in this same seat on the way to the hospital. I shook free from the memory of Dad's hurtful words. This was my first homecoming. I hoped we could leave the battlefield behind. Things were different now. I was different now.

Sleep came quickly, and so did the dawn.

"Mom! Dad! Wake up! There's a soldier out here!" The voice of my younger brother snapped through my morning sleep, much like reveille did back at the barracks.

I jumped out of the car ready to stand at attention, only to find my brother bent over in laughter. I'm not sure which one of us scared the other more. I joined in the fun, flicking the back of my brother's head, and then I ran toward the backyard.

"Freto! I'm home, boy!" Wiping back a tear, I leaned in to pet my furry friend. I hadn't realized how badly I needed a Freto fix!

All the food they serve you in the army comes from a can. There were days I would have given anything for some fresh Blue Lake string beans from my dad's garden, even if I had to pick them myself. So I especially enjoyed breakfast that morning in my mom's kitchen.

SNARES EXPOSED

But suddenly, I choked back the weight of expectation my dad heaped on me as a kid. I began to wonder whether he ever really noticed I had been gone. Did he miss me? Would he ever say so?

The awkward silence that once provided a good hiding place no longer covered me. Rather, it exposed me. It exposed my father's hesitation to receive the man now sitting across the table from him. His eyes followed my every move. His words hung in the shadows, and I wondered whether he might be sizing up my weaknesses. I wished he would comment on my strengths.

Maybe he didn't see them. Maybe he saw them and chose not to fortify them with the power of his words. Instead, his silence spoke with authority. And I battled against the lies I heard reinforced by that authority for most of my years.

Me. Ray Sturt. Expert sharpshooter.

Ignorant and unworthy.

CHAPTER 3

AN EMERGING ALLIANCE

*In his heart a man plans his course,
but the LORD determines his steps.*
—Proverbs 16:9

Exposed, yet ever determined to work hard, I returned to Fort Dix for the final months of training. Those last days were grueling. In the end, my comrades and I graduated boot camp and parted ways.

A majority of them shipped off to Vietnam, and many lost their lives. Vietnam must have been a hard place to fight and an especially hard place to die. Controversy concerning the war filled the newspapers. The country seemed divided, families torn, many people angry to have to sacrifice for something so awful that seemed so pointless.

"This is not a jungle war, but a struggle for freedom on every front of human activity." Lyndon B. Johnson's words echoed across the country, reminding us all of the value of freedom. But the cost was high.

I heard stories. Terrible stories. Stories that could barely be told to another living soul. The enemy, vicious, often invisible, hiding in the bush, waiting like an animal to devour young men. Battle lines often blurred. Becoming difficult to identify in the dense vegetation. Alliances formed, but in this hostile environment, it was pretty much every man for himself.

I didn't know then that one day I would be engaged in a jungle war not so different from the one in Vietnam.

My whole life, I hid as far away from the front line as I could get. Today it's called strategic planning. At times, I knew the guilt of being alive when so many of my comrades were not. I served my six-year duty to Uncle Sam without having to engage in hand-to-hand combat in the Vietnam jungles.

After six character-building months at Fort Dix, I wound up stationed at Fort Lee, just a mile from my parents' home in Virginia. Mom hoped I would help her take care of the business on my days off, but I had my own way of doing things now. I needed adventure, and I knew where to find it.

Much to my mom's disappointment, I returned to the big city of Newport News and rented a room from a nice widowed lady. Close enough to commute to Fort Lee for my weekends of reserve duty, I was able to continue the machinist training I began at the shipbuilding company before being sent to Fort Dix.

Every day on my way to the shipyard, a good mile's walk, I thought about the same kinds of questions that used to come to mind while I sat on the picnic table in my backyard. Important questions, pondering the universe and my place in it. Wondering if I would ever know love. Real love. Hoping that someday my life would matter—like the soldiers fighting in Vietnam. Giving your life so that other human beings would know freedom? That was a life that mattered. Maybe one day I would be willing to sacrifice my life for someone else's freedom.

Meanwhile, I discovered I made significant contributions in other ways. The Newport News Shipbuilding and Dry Dock Company received orders for work no other yard could manage, even nuclear submarines! While I never worked on anything nuclear, I did enjoy the privilege of contributing to parts that went into building the aircraft carrier *John F. Kennedy*. A picture of Jacqueline Kennedy and her family hung in the lobby near the president's office. Her daughter, Caroline, actually broke a bottle of champagne against the hull of the ship, christening it with her father's name. The JFK carrier was a big deal.

Me. Ray Sturt. Contributing to a big deal. I liked the sound of that.

Working at a shipyard, I heard lots of things I wished I hadn't. Sometimes I said stuff just to shock people when they were bugging me with their language or behavior. But in spite of having been in the army, I was still a quiet kind of fellow. One afternoon, when every word out of a guy's mouth cursed the name of God, I called his girlfriend a hussy.

Taught me to keep my mouth shut, I'll tell ya! The guy liked to have ripped my head off! He only stopped when he realized I had the same kind of respect for God that he had for his girlfriend. I guess I carried something for the Lord that went deeper than I knew. Or maybe He carried something deeper for me than I knew.

Either way, there were people who saw the potential of Christ in me. Like my landlady. Just about every weekend, she invited me to come to her gospel-believing church down at the corner. "I know the Lord has something special in mind for you, Ray Sturt," she would say. For me? Ray Sturt? I hoped so. I always hoped so. But I always declined her invitation. I couldn't be held back on the weekends. I had places to go and a sweet ride to get me there!

My 1967 Ford Mustang made me feel as if I were a kid roaming the roads on my bike again. I so loved taking my car out cruising through the countryside. She was made for the road. Her wide, low body hugged a curb like nobody's business. Every weekend, we drove the one-hour trip back to Petersburg together. We were a good pair. She let me talk as much as I wanted. I let her zip past anything that was moving too slow!

To this day, I'm not sure why I went to Mom and Dad's even when I didn't have reserve duty, but I did. Maybe I wanted to give Dad a chance for positive conversation, or maybe I just needed clean laundry. Whatever the reason, we always ended up going to church together, just like we did when I was a boy. Dad made sure of it. The only reason I went, though, was to please him. I guess I thought it would gain me points, or something. Or maybe he would like me better if I didn't fight him on stuff.

I left church every week feeling about the same as when I went in: empty. Unchallenged to think deeply about my faith or to make a real connection with the Lord, I continued to believe the only real Christians were the apostles and a couple of missionaries I knew who sold everything they had and moved to foreign countries. Maybe my perspective was distorted by my perception of my dad's church attendance. He went every week, but he was not the same man at church that he was at home. At church, he was charismatic and happy toward everybody, especially the preacher, but even to the old man who walked with his head down and never cracked a smile. It made it hard for me to trust preachers or my dad. Why would I take to heart something a man said who let people put him on a pedestal?

I'm telling you the truth. That kind of double life never did appeal to me. It didn't feel honest to me even to go to church sometimes. But I went. Maybe one day something would make sense. I knew God protected me, and somehow I understood He had a plan for my life. I guess, for the time being, it had to be enough.

Except that ... well, it really wasn't enough. Working hard, for me, was a way to feel alive and useful. But when break times came, it wasn't work I wanted to pursue. I wanted to find love. Settle down. Marry a nice girl to take care of me and have a family with. The truth is, I had no idea how. All I knew was to do what my father said to do. This making-my-way thing may not have been working as well as I'd hoped. It wasn't the romantic life I had envisioned. I struggled. In school, at work, in life.

I left Newport News on the weekends because I didn't know how to stay in Newport News. Odd, isn't it? A guy like me, strong and hard working, running home to Mom and Dad? Like they were going to give me what I was missing. I'm sure nobody ever noticed I had left. I didn't mind so much. There were worse places to hide than in a slick new Mustang!

AN EMERGING ALLIANCE

Eventually, it became too hard to stay in Newport News. Period. I couldn't manage being on the front line of this battlefield. I knew an emptiness that pounded away on my heart. In spite of really wanting to make a go of life on my own, I went home.

While I no longer wanted to live by myself in the city, and I still served in the reserves at Fort Lee, I wanted to pursue a career as a machinist. Something about the precision work appealed to me. It was manageable. Predictable. The same every time as long as I followed the right path to achieve the measurements, often within slim tolerances of 0.0005. So I transferred credits from the shipyard apprentice school and enrolled in night classes at the Petersburg Vocational Trade School.

After four years of study, working full time at Titmus Optical during the day and getting in eight thousand hours of shop experience, I graduated. Now, what do you think about that? Me. Ray Sturt. A graduate certified by the state as a journeyman machinist by trade. No matter how many times I had wanted to quit, I didn't. And there I stood with a certificate in my hand.

Maybe my patience at working hard and getting through hard times had paid off. One of Grandpa Sturt's favorite cowboy sayings went like this: "You can't tell how a good man or a watermelon is 'til they get thumped." I was hoping, with all this thumping over the years, that someone might finally see me. A good man. Smart. Respectable. Worthy.

In the middle of figuring out all that life stuff, I managed to escape now and again for a little fun. The company I worked for sponsored two duckpin bowling teams that played in a league every Monday night. Coed.

This wasn't your normal, everyday, ten-pin sport. Duckpins are shorter than regular bowling pins. Squattier, and a lot lighter. And the ball? Well, you hold the ball in the palm of your hand. It may seem like an easy kid's game, but it's not. Just like in ten-pin bowling, the object is to get all the pins down in one roll. It is impossible! For a perfect game, you have to get a strike on each of twelve rolls in a row, for three hundred points. I don't believe anyone has ever done it. But it sure was a lot of fun trying.

A natural athlete, I picked up on the skill fairly easily. A few times I thought I might have a chance to shoot for three hundred, but a few stubborn pins always seemed to stand in my way. It seemed that the rest of the team did well when I bowled well, so I always tried extra hard. In the end, we all pulled together and wound up winning the play-off tournament at the end of the season!

The league put together a banquet to celebrate our victory. Everyone planned to come, and most everybody had a date. I refused to be the only one without a date. Maybe this would be the open door I needed to find the love of my life. After all, aren't champion athletes every girl's dream?

After days of getting up my nerve, I called a girl a friend had introduced me to. Crossing my fingers behind my back, I hoped she had heard about my athleticism and good manners. The conversation went well, and we made a plan. I had a date!

On the night of the banquet, I pulled up outside her door in my sporty Mustang. She was a very nice-looking young lady. I met her at the door and put on my very best behavior. I opened all the doors as we came to them, pulled out her chair, and made polite conversation. I even served her drinks. The banquet lived up to its high-end billing, including a steak dinner with all the trimmings. Afterward, each of us on the winning duckpin team walked to the stage to receive a trophy for our accomplishments. Everybody clapped and laughed and seemed to be enjoying a good time—except for my date. She was polite and very quiet the whole night. Evidently, she was not impressed by my champion athlete status.

After the banquet, we drove back to her apartment in silence. I wondered whether she might be hiding there in the awkwardness like I used to do. Remembering, I graciously walked around the car, opened her door, and escorted her to the front porch. Without saying a word, my date slipped inside, closed the door behind her and left me in a state of disbelief. Not a word. Not even a thank-you.

Furious, I beelined it back to the car, revved the engine, and peeled from her driveway as if I were getting a jump start at a drag strip. I must have laid thirty feet of rubber on the street in front of her apartment that night. How embarrassing. She couldn't even say thank you? There was no way I could go home. And face my dad? I'd rather crawl under the shed. So I hid in my car for a while, driving and yelling, sitting and thinking. My quest for love wasn't going very well. Not at all.

I wondered whether I would ever have a chance to know love. Who would ever want to spend her life with me? Ray Sturt. Awkward. Naïve.

As I sat there in my car, mustering the courage to go inside the house, it dawned on me that maybe I had a handicap. A relational handicap. I didn't know how to treat a girl. I never learned. With the way my father treated my mother, I didn't have a very good role model. They didn't express love toward each other, let alone to us. It hadn't struck me like that before. I'm not sure I ever saw them kiss. In the quiet of my car, I wished out loud for a miracle. And I didn't even really know what a miracle was. But I knew I needed help and that God had some kind of pull in such things. *Please, God, bring me a wife. Someday. Somehow. Somebody who can love me.*

Mom knew how to soothe her young man's heart. When I got home the night of the disastrous date, she scooped us some ice cream and pulled up a chair for a chat. We talked late into the night about how I might go about finding a wife.

"Ray, you'll find somebody," she reassured me. I nodded my head in response, but my insides shook like a leaf in a stormy wind.

Mom helped spread the word that I needed to find a wife. Soon, everyone wanted in on the act. From every corner of the family, I started receiving invitations to meet girls. "She's a lovely girl," Aunt Mary said. "Your cousin knows her from school."

Nice, someone familiar, sort of. I felt at ease about asking this girl to go with me to a movie. We enjoyed each other's company. The girl seemed very friendly toward me. I needed somebody who could be friendly. After a few days, I received a phone call from my aunt.

"Ray, watch that girl," she said. "She thinks your family rolls in money." Evidently, my date had asked my cousin a thousand questions about our family business. How many trailers? Who runs everything? I couldn't believe how much she already knew and how much digging she had done. I did not ask this girl out again. Imagine, a gold digger trying to snag me? My dad owned a mobile home park, not a home on Park Avenue.

Every day, it seemed, someone told me about another girl I should meet or invited me over to meet someone they knew. Some of those meetings did not go very well. One night, after enjoying dinner in the home of a Baptist minister, I asked whether I could take their daughter to see the Disney movie *Black Beauty*. Her mom stood back and looked at me as though I had two heads. "We do NOT attend any movies of any kind," she responded in her no-nonsense, I'm-the-mom-and-what-I-say-goes voice. Right then and there I called her out on a technicality.

"Ma'am," I said, trying to be polite, "if that were true, you would have to throw that television straight out the window!"

She didn't like that I talked to her that way, even though I spoke the truth. We were watching a movie on television that very minute! I left pretty directly after that. No sense in staying.

"Those religious people are all hypocrites," I told my mom. I meant it. I didn't ask that girl out again, either.

I needed to expand my search. Being a man of integrity and adhering to Christian values, though I wasn't yet a Christian, I knew I wanted a Christian wife. Surely, if I visited churches other than my own, I would find more available girls to my liking. One Sunday I attended the evening service of a church in another part of town.

When the last song ended, I caught a young lady out of the corner of my eye. She seemed to be coming my way in a hurry, so I stepped back

AN EMERGING ALLIANCE

out of her way. As I did, this slender young woman with long, wavy blonde hair positioned herself right up close to my side and extended her hand toward mine. "You're new here," she said in a quiet voice. "Hi. I'm Betty." We talked for a while, and she invited me to follow her home, where we sat on the couch and talked for another hour or two. I thought we might be hitting it off. Then Betty asked if I wanted to go for a walk. In the dark. To the cemetery. I can tell you that she did not want me to follow her to the cemetery so she could introduce me to her great-grandfather. Somehow, Betty thought that I was the kind of guy who wanted more from a girl than just to talk on the couch. It was all I could do not to slam the door in her face and run. Very far away. She did not know me. Me. Ray Sturt. Quiet. Naïve. Making out in the cemetery?

I made my way home instead, glad for morals and wondering where to find a girl who shared the same principles. Going to church had gotten me nowhere.

Determined, I stepped up the intensity. I refused to go through life alone. Little did I know how important that tenacity and intention would be down the road.

Several weeks and failed dates later, I called on a young lady I met through a mutual friend. A nursing student, she was at the top of her class. Beautiful, smart, and kind. As a special treat, I arranged for us to take a day trip to the vacation home my parents had purchased on Lake Gaston. It would be good to get away from studies, work, and stress for a day of tranquility, basking by the lake, and taking leisurely walks.

On a gorgeous, sunny morning, we took off. My plans, innocent and meant to be a gift, turned sour quickly. My date did not have pure intentions. Once we arrived, she turned on her charm and later tried to lead me into the woods.

I was done.

I promptly took the girl home, only to find her boyfriend waiting for us in the driveway. Her boyfriend? The string of nastiness that exploded from his mouth made me want to vomit. "Get in my car, *#*#*#!" he bellowed. "We need to have ourselves a little conversation."

I refused, quietly walking around the front of my car to open the door for my date. On the outside, I'm sure I looked calm and in control—maybe even brave. But on the inside, I wished I could run. Very far away. Very fast.

"You can have her," I replied. And I meant it.

The girl had the nerve to call me when I got home. "I'm sorry," she said. I could practically hear her eyelashes flirting my direction. "Hank is a real jealous guy. He said I'd better not see you again, or else …" Good riddance.

Now I was really done.

Until my dad decided to get involved. "Son …" (Oh boy, here we go. I don't say no to my dad.) "Now I know you wanted that girl for yourself. Though I don't know what you saw in her. She even made my feathers flop. You know, she ain't the only fish in the pond." Dad went on to tell me about Mandy, a home economist who worked in the same office building he did. As he talked, I could see that he approved of this girl. I agreed to give her a try. After all, she had a college degree and a great job! How bad could it be?

Evidently, not bad at all! Mandy and I began a long-term relationship. I even traded my 1967 Ford Mustang for a nice-looking baby-blue LTD sedan, complete with whitewalls and a vinyl top so that I could court her in style. I quickly began hoping that Mandy was the one for me. I didn't touch her for a whole three months! We didn't kiss or even hold hands. We spent every Friday night together for weeks and weeks. Bowling, watching a movie, or dancing at the Battlefield Park Swim and Raquet Club. Some Fridays we simply sat in a quiet place and enjoyed each other's company. I could talk to Mandy for hours.

On Saturdays, Mandy drove up to Richmond to visit overnight with relatives there. Every Saturday. Every weekend. While I went with her on a couple of occasions, over the course of a year Mandy didn't choose to stay home for even one weekend with me. I worked hard to spend my available time with her, even making time on the weekends when I had reserve duty. She was important to me. I took every bit of overtime I could get in order to put money away for our future. But I began to question how she felt about me. And some things happened that caused me to question her moral character.

We were done. I wanted a wife of strong character. Someone who lived by the same high principles I tried to live by. Did someone like that exist for me? Someone who could eventually become my partner for life?

I wondered whether love might require something more than hard work. But I knew only hard work. Discouragement overwhelmed me. In a moment of surrender, I removed myself from the front line, quietly served out the remainder of my duty in the reserves, and threw myself back into my job. I took every hour of work offered to me and invested in U.S. savings bonds.

On April 17, 1972, I received an honorable discharge from the United States Army Reserves. There was no big graduation ceremony like there was at the end of boot camp, but I received a nice document officially declaring my release. My father seemed proud. He didn't say so, but he shook my hand. Not in a father-to-young-son sort of way, but in a man-to-man sort of way.

Still, in spite of the acknowledgement of serving in something as important as the army, loneliness consumed me. Imagine. Me, a veteran trained for combat with an M-16, crying myself to sleep more nights than I care to say. Most nights this prayer burst from my lips, "Please, God, have mercy on me. Give me a wife!"

"In his heart a man plans his course, but the LORD determines his steps" (Prov. 16:9). I had no idea just how determined the Lord could be. I didn't know Him at the time, and I didn't know He had His providential hand on me. In every relationship, through every conversation, holding me securely, handling every situation.

On May 13, 1972, a woman walked into my dad's recovery room at the John Randolph Hospital and flipped my perspective on life. Forever. Situated in the small industrial town of Hopewell, Virginia, John Randolph was the closest hospital to Petersburg without running to the big city. I don't know to this day why Dad had his hernia surgery there instead of in Petersburg. But he did. And I was glad, even though we used to jokingly refer to the town as "HopeLESS Well," saying nothing good could ever come from there. But that night proved me wrong.

Something good did come from Hopewell, and I followed her all the way back to the nurse's station. Dressed in white clear to her toes and wearing a starched nurse's cap atop her head, Linda looked pretty as an angel. "Pardon me, Nurse Linda," I said nervously as she worked her way behind the counter. "I was wondering if you would like to go to a movie or something sometime … with me." She looked up at me with her sweet brown eyes and before she could speak, I went right on. "I have a nice new LTD sedan with whitewalls and everything. And I have a boat too. I like to ski. Sometimes I like to just go out on the lake in my boat and—"

Nurse Linda stopped me right there. "Yes," she said quietly. Her lips curved in a gentle smile as she interrupted my rush of words. Every ounce of shyness I had had since I was a boy gurgled straight to my head, right in that moment. I looked down for a second to compose myself, and off she went to see her next patient, leaving me to recover from my awkwardness.

A big smile made its way across my face as I walked back toward Dad's room. It was such an unusual look for me those days that my mom asked, "What have you gotten yourself into now, Ray Sturt?" The tone in her voice took me back to the days when I would come running into the kitchen from outside, with blackberry juice dripping from my chin and running straight down my shirtsleeve.

"She said yes," I stammered.

Mom just grinned. "Of course she did, Ray. Of course she did."

AN EMERGING ALLIANCE

The days that followed our meeting moved liked a snail. I watched for Nurse Linda every chance I got. If I saw her, but she didn't see me, I would lean back against the wall and linger as long as she remained in my line of sight. Friday couldn't come fast enough.

When it finally arrived, I hoped for the life of me that it wasn't a dream. After seeing a movie, Linda and I sat at Shoney's enjoying fresh strawberry pie and getting to know one another until two o'clock in the morning! On our first date! If we had been dreaming, surely one of us would have woke up by then! It was real, all right. And we were having the time of our lives—just sitting! We seemed to be drawn together by some sort of special force.

Eventually, the evening drew to a close, and I drove Linda home. I can remember, plain as day, Linda taking my hand when I opened the passenger door of my sedan that night. It was as if we had been in that very same spot before. I may not have been dreaming at the time, but this was the woman I'd been dreaming of my entire life.

A sense of assurance I had never before experienced settled in on me. I wondered whether God might be answering my prayer. Before long, I would have my answer. In the light of day, I would be undone by how quickly He moved and how completely He knew my needs before I uttered a single word.

Summer came upon us, and I put Linda through the test. The "lake test." On her days off in the Sunday school teaching rotation, we loaded up my LTD with everything we might need for a day of hiking, boating, skiing, swimming, and eating with my parents down at their place on Gaston. Linda didn't swim, which caused me concern at first. But she made up for it by driving the boat so I could ski. Let me tell you, she had no clue how to drive a boat! But she did it—slalom style! She slammed headfirst into every wave she found and skipped me like a stone across every wake. Linda, the girl of my dreams, carried herself in a manner of utmost gentleness until she got behind the wheel. Out from under her sweet exterior, playfulness emerged. Strong and full of vigor. She took great delight in trying to dump me!

Somewhere in the wooded surroundings of Lake Gaston, the ache of loneliness faded and friendship emerged. True friendship; grounded in goodness. As we walked along the dusty roads, we took care in revealing family secrets and entrusting our souls to one another. These conversations at the lake poured a foundation for our growing relationship. Neither of us could have anticipated just how essential that foundation would become for our survival in the future.

From the very beginning, Linda submitted to the plans I came up with for our dates. She cared more about the quality of our time together than she did about the amount of money I spent. No pressure! We enjoyed doing a lot of the same activities: riding bikes, jogging, serving others in need. So we simply did them together. I mean to tell you, I thought the day would never come that I would meet a woman who wanted to jog with me. Me. Ray Sturt. We even washed our cars together and had a ball doing it!

My dear Linda brought out the best in me, though she would say that we encouraged and believed in the best for each other. She put aside expectations based on her previous dating experiences and allowed me to take the lead in our blossoming relationship. She poured out kindness toward me, demonstrating her love as if it were an aggressive goodwill. Only someone who knew Christ could show love as unselfishly as Linda showed it. I had never experienced this kind of love before.

I began to see Linda as a potential partner, someone with whom I could build a life. But my parents began to question the emerging alliance.

"I never pegged you to go out with such a religious fanatic," my father said to me after a day at the lake. "You're spending so much time together, she's gonna rub off on you. What will you do then?" He was unnerved at the thought of losing control.

AN EMERGING ALLIANCE

He did not unnerve me.

Ironically, Dad happened to be one of the tools God used to bring Linda and me together by His divine providence. If Dad's surgery had been at Petersburg General, where he normally received care, and not in Hopewell, I would never have met Linda. That's why Linda and I always say that God, alone, introduced us.

Now here's a surprise that my father never knew. Linda started "rubbing off on me" the moment I laid eyes on her. In fact, she got quickly under my skin. Linda, on the other hand, had to exercise her faith in order to say yes to me. After dating several young men while in her early twenties, she became frustrated and resigned herself to life without a partner. She wasn't anxious to get back on the dating roller coaster. But, she reasoned after our first night out, "Why not try dating this guy? What do I have to lose?" With God's help, she took the risk and began practicing sacrificial, submissive love. Because of Linda, I came to know the depth of Christ's love expressed. Being a witness to Linda's life made me want to know Christ more.

Without really knowing Him, I had been carrying an awareness of Christ's presence and protection in my life for a long time. Mercifully, He stuck with me. My time to respond to him would be only a short distance down the road. Linda would be instrumental, though she didn't see it at the time. She knew of my search for more meaning than I found in the empty religion at my church. But she didn't yet know the depth of the stirring or my need to respond.

Being a man whose identity hinged on hard work, I enjoyed my job as a machinist for the Titmus Optical Company. I kept my head down and did with excellence what had to be done. I took breaks at the allotted times, usually alone. I appreciated the quiet and the space to think. It was as if I were a kid again, sitting on my parents' backyard picnic table. I pondered life and the wonder of love to fill up life. Lately I had been considering Christ and wondered whether He might be proud of the way I lived. That question tugged at me more often than I let on.

One afternoon a fellow machinist came and sat with me for a while. We talked a little. Then he slipped a small red booklet into one hand as he shook the other. "Ray, it's been good getting to know you a little better," he said. "Take a look at this when you get the chance. I think you might like what you find."

Curious, I flipped quickly through the printed pages as the whistle blew to return to the floor. I shoved the booklet deep into the back pocket of my dungarees, wanting to be sure it didn't fall out. This small gift could well turn out to be a great treasure.

In my constant search for meaning, I decided to attend church with Linda regularly. There seemed to always be something new. I mentioned my amazement quite a lot, which surprised Linda. But it was so different from the church where Dad took us growing up. People smiled and hugged. They expressed concern and prayed for one another, right in the middle of the hallway! While we were painting!

I really had never had so much fun in a church building as the Saturday afternoon when Linda and I helped a group of young adults do some painting. I wondered what my dad would say. Maybe he would call me a fanatic? If so, he would be at least partly right. I was a fan of this church, and though I had not yet given my life to the Lord, I was happy to serve.

As the summer heat began to dissipate, the church hosted an evangelistic crusade. Walking into the building that night with Linda, the energy in the air captured me immediately. Music poured from the piano, inviting us into the auditorium for worship. I never sang so much on one night in my entire life! The guest soloist presented some exceptional music, and the pastor delivered a powerful presentation of the gospel. After he spoke, lots of people went to the front of the room to receive prayer, and many responded to the invitation to receive Christ. I wondered whether I should walk up there too, but I was too shy. Linda brought me out of a lot of shyness with her sparkling personality, but I still liked to hide in crowds of people. She understood

AN EMERGING ALLIANCE

my shyness. I was learning to love that about my Linda. She knew how to let me be me. Ray Sturt.

As we got into my car after the service, Linda turned and asked, "What did you get out of that wonderful church service, Ray?" I felt a little on the spot and started to fidget with my keys. I told her I liked the music and the happiness everybody seemed to carry around. Then I put the keys down, reached for the red booklet of verses from my wallet, and turned to look into the sweetest face on the earth.

"Linda, I have a confession." My voice shook slightly, but only for a second. "I wanted to go forward during the invitation, but I felt too embarrassed. I have never received Christ." I went on to tell her about the booklet and offered insight into how I could attend church most of my life and still not have a real relationship with Christ. She nodded gently and reached over to take my hand at one point. Oh, how I loved the tenderness of this woman's spirit.

I already knew I was a sinner and that I could do nothing to save myself. I had gone to church for years with my family and watched Billy Graham crusades on television more than once. But that night, for the first time, I saw that Jesus died specifically for me. Me. Ray Sturt. What do you think about that? I began to read aloud. "That if thou shalt confess with thy mouth the Lord Jesus, and shalt believe in thine heart that God hath raised Him from the dead, thou shalt be saved. For with the heart man believeth unto righteousness; and with the mouth confession is made unto salvation" (Rom. 10:9–10 KJV).

Right then, the Spirit of God came upon me, and I understood and believed. With Linda holding my hand, I bowed my head and prayed silently in my heart. *God, please forgive me. I am a sinner in need of Your mercy. I believe Your Son, Jesus, died for me and that His precious blood washes me clean from all my sin. By faith I ask Him to come into my heart and be the Lord of my life. Thank You for saving me. Amen.* When I looked up from my prayer, Linda was smiling. So was I.

"I finally did it! I gave my life to Jesus!"

Linda squeezed my hand. "I'm so proud to be sitting here with you."

Her soft-spoken words held me through many hard days in the years to come. An alliance was emerging. A truly blessed alliance.

CHAPTER 4

AN ESTABLISHED HOME FRONT

Home is where one starts from.
—T. S. Eliot

On November 23, 1972, Linda and I committed to a lifetime alliance, grounded in faith, bound in love, united in holy matrimony. With one hundred fifty friends and family as witnesses, we celebrated that Thanksgiving Day like none before. God, in His abundant mercy, showed Himself faithful in answering our fervent prayers. At three o'clock in the afternoon, after all the gobblers had been stuffed and panned, Linda's pastor led us in a ceremony where we vowed to be together "until death do us part."

What do you think about that? Me. Ray Sturt. Married to the most amazing woman on the face of the earth. We were in love. This union was right and most everyone agreed. In that moment, I didn't believe death would ever come between us, though it would threaten to.

After whisking my bride away for a weeklong honeymoon in Florida, we returned to Petersburg to establish our life together as a married couple. The beginning days of our union were not without challenges. We moved into a trailer I owned and parked at my parents' mobile home park. Being that close to my dad could become a little tense. But

Linda and I counted every moment we had together as a blessing and turned our little bungalow into a very comfortable home.

Knowing that we wanted our marriage to be grounded in faith, we immediately began reading Scripture out loud to each other every day. By the time our first anniversary came around, we had read through the entire Bible! As a new Christian, I was like a sponge. I wanted a deep and personal relationship with Christ, so if the church doors were open, I was there. My hunger for the Word of God grew to astounding levels. Every opportunity I had, I had my nose in Scripture. Reading, remembering, memorizing. Linda marveled at my enthusiasm and joined me whenever we could be together.

Soon we found ourselves wanting to serve. It's how we're wired. We went to see our pastor, who took us straight into Scripture. Deuteronomy 24:5 commands that a soldier be exempt from war and other duties during the first year of his marriage. This released him from outside responsibilities in order to strengthen his marriage and bring happiness to his new wife. It allowed time for a spiritual and physical bond to develop between them. The pastor followed up his explanation with, "So I recommend that you take a year off from serving in the church. It will give you opportunity to learn to leave your families and cleave to one another."

I wondered whether my ears needed cleaning. Did he just say that we couldn't serve the Lord for a whole year? Peering across his desk, watching us squirm, the pastor grinned. "Ah, I'm just kidding. In what area would you like to serve?" I'll tell you, he really had us going. He did strongly suggest that we do something together and asked us to check in with him occasionally. I guess he wanted to be sure we cleaved properly.

Linda and I both felt relief. We could imagine no greater joy than serving the Lord together. It was a natural expression of our love for one another and our mutual love for the Lord and His Word.

The pastor helped us consider our options for ministry. It was hard to narrow in on one thing, but he could see my enthusiasm and natural ability to reach out to people. We both so wanted to share the peace and joy of Christ with others. "Ray, do you still keep up your chauffeur's license?" Linda asked with a glint in her eye.

AN ESTABLISHED HOME FRONT

"The church has a bus," the pastor immediately chimed in. "And we could use a bus pastor. What if you picked people up for church on Sunday?"

Linda and I both leaned toward him at the same time with a concerted, "YES!" Now we were getting somewhere. I was going to be a bus pastor!

As plans worked themselves out, I took Saturday afternoons to study the Bible and memorize verses. Then I went into the community of Hopewell to visit people in their homes. They were hungry for attention, and I gave it to them, clothed in the mercy and strength of the Lord. I shared the love of Christ with them by listening to their stories and encouraging them with Scripture and prayer. Linda came with me sometimes. With her gift of mercy, how special those afternoons were for us and for the people we visited! The Lord's faithfulness grew in me by leaps and bounds in my early years as a Christian. I couldn't imagine a time when I would ever withhold from Him anything within me.

All kinds of people rode with us to church on the bus every week. We picked up small children, big children, older adults, and younger adults. We even picked up Linda's parents! What do you think about that? They had always called a taxi to get to church because they never owned a car or had a driver's license. Oh, what a blessing Sunday mornings came to be. We sang praise songs, talked about the Bible, and I recited Scriptures of encouragement and salvation. Linda often baked cookies or other kinds of treats. We passed out tracts and donuts and even hot chocolate when the air was chilly.

What a contrast my life had become compared to what I had endured as a kid. The way Linda loved me showed up in so many wonderful places. She was the apple of my eye. My delight. My lover and my friend. She even found me a new job at the Aqualon factory, where she worked briefly as a nurse.

I couldn't imagine life getting any sweeter, being any more complete—until the delivery-room nurse placed our son, Scott, in my stiff, outstretched arms for the very first time.

How could one so small warm such a heart as mine?

Me. Ray Sturt. A dad. What do you think about that? I wondered whether my son would ever know how big my heart felt the first time I looked into his eyes, felt his fingers curl around mine? I watched a tear drop onto Scott's squishy red face. In that moment, I knew my life wasn't about me or about Linda.

I was so proud of that boy, even before he did a single thing to deserve it. I hoped I always would be. And that I would tell him. No matter what. If holding your son for the first time doesn't humble a man, I don't know what will. I prayed a prayer, asking God to help me walk worthy of a son who belonged to Him.

Linda and I loved the blessing of including Scott in our lives. He came to us before our first anniversary, which limited our time for blending as a couple. But being a family of three gave us growing opportunities. Our gift was from the Lord, and it was right.

Before his first birthday, Scott stepped into his role as associate bus pastor. I carried my little "peanut" with me into many homes on Saturday afternoons. People welcomed us, accepting us in the same way we accepted them whatever activity they were involved in, no matter the clothes they wore or the messiness of their home. In some of the underprivileged areas where we ministered, children ran in and out of the house while I shared spiritual truths from Scripture. They were filthy from playing outside all hours of the day and running everywhere without supervision. But those things didn't matter. We went every week to offer encouragement and show the concern of Christ, no matter the circumstances. If no one came to the door, I followed up later with a phone call. Most of these people genuinely looked forward to our visit every week, especially after Scott came along. He was quite the young ambassador, an essential member of the Sturt team.

As our homefront stabilized, the Sturts stepped into expanded service opportunities in the church. Elected as a deacon, my responsibilities increased. I took none of them lightly, and anything we did, we did as a family. United in the Spirit.

Maintaining the church property kept us deacons the busiest. We mowed grass regularly and often took care of the cleaning. We also took up and counted the offering every week. Twice I got to give my

AN ESTABLISHED HOME FRONT

testimony during the church service. But greeting people before church became one of my favorite duties. "Welcome. It's good to see you this morning," I would say as I handed them a bulletin. Then I ushered each family to a pew inside the sanctuary while Linda waited for me in our usual spot.

She was my biggest support and the love of my life. I'm telling you, she sure lit up a room. Anyone who sat near us sure knew it too, especially the newcomers. With her warm smile, she made everyone feel that they belonged.

The Lord really smiled on me the day she walked into my dad's hospital room. I'm telling the truth about that. I don't know where I'd be without her and God. I know I wouldn't be where I am, and that's about all there is to know.

※

In the summer of 1976, the year our nation celebrated her bicentennial birthday, the Lord expanded our family with the addition of another amazing child. Adam was born on June 11, two years and nine months after Scott and three pounds heavier. When the nurse handed him to me, I stroked his head in wonderment. Every hair placed there was the work of the Lord. I wondered what I had done to deserve one son; now I had the blessing of two. My heart filled with pride as I looked Adam in the eye and saw the heart of a mighty warrior. "Oh, God, thank you for trusting me, Ray Sturt, to be the father of such a miracle," I prayed. "Help me to walk worthy of a son who belongs to You."

※

Adam grew quickly, in size and in strength. Every day when I stepped into his room after work, he greeted me from his crib, lying on his belly and pushing his head up as high as he could. Sometimes I waited for a minute in the doorway until he got his head around to catch my eye with the twinkle in his. My little Turtlehead. What a delight.

And what a load! Adam weighed in at thirty pounds before he could walk and before he was old enough to be out of his crib. But I wouldn't have traded him for anything. Adam was the perfect, God-ordained addition to our family. Essential in every way. We would come to rely on Adam's strength. A strength uniquely his to use for the benefit of the Lord's kingdom.

As our boys grew, Linda and I grew more and more grateful for the home the Lord provided. A tri-level in Chester, Virginia, with a large yard perfect for the boys to romp in, sat at the crossroad hub of the neighborhood. It became the perfect place to strengthen our bonds and use our unique abilities by opening ourselves toward other families. As soon as they were old enough, Scott and Adam began inviting friends over. Lots of friends. Especially neighbors and later school buddies.

Recognizing the mission that it could become, we wanted our home to be a safe place for kids to play. As a family, we wanted them to feel welcome. Linda and I wanted to build relationships with the kids' parents too. So many seemed stretched to their limits. It was a good ministry for us and for our boys. And what a compliment to be entrusted with the care of another's child! Though we spent a lot of afternoons refereeing squabbles over toys and spilling a lot of energy entertaining everyone, we wouldn't have traded those times for anything. They strengthened our ability to be the family God called us to be. The more we played, the more we bonded.

Days would come when resistance would press that bond to its limit. God knew what He was doing. We trusted Him, without question, as a couple. And we were growing that trust in our boys.

With all the maneuvering and hiding I did as a boy, I still managed to take away some good skills from my dad that helped me later in life. Linda and I wanted to influence our sons with good Christian music,

AN ESTABLISHED HOME FRONT

so I wired a speaker for each of their bedrooms. We had no idea the foundation we were giving the boys, as they both developed musical abilities far beyond what we could ever have imagined.

I also constructed a swing and a sandbox in the backyard with some leftover pipes and metal sheeting to give the boys and their friends more to do outside. They both seemed to enjoy sharing the things I made with their friends. One afternoon, I overheard a younger boy ask where they got the cool sandbox. He wanted one too. Adam responded, "My dad made it. He's the best builder in the whole entire universe. If you're nice to me, maybe he'll make you one too!" That boy. Always teasing like his dad.

I wondered whether I had ever bragged about something my dad did for me. Nothing came to mind right away, so I tucked that thought in my back pocket for a day when I needed something to think about.

With two active boys at home, I didn't get as much time for thinking as I once did. But I didn't mind. I would rather hang out with them, anyway, which I did a lot. Two nights a week, while Linda worked the afternoon shift at the hospital, I picked the boys up from Grandma's when I got off work. Then we went home to make one of my three special gourmet meals. Scott and Adam took turns picking from the menu: pizza and applesauce, hot dogs with pork and beans, or fish sticks with green peas and applesauce. To this day we joke about that extensive meal plan! But we had what we needed, and the most important "meal" was our laughter and time together.

After dinner we dug out board games or tore up the living room. Now, before you question a father with such a lack of discipline, you need to know that our living room was a special place—a furniture-free zone! We kept the room empty on purpose to give the boys space to be boys, all the way into their teenage years. The thick, comfy carpet made it the perfect place for tumbling, tickling, and chasing. Some nights they like to have killed me with their two-on-one wrestling matches. But every ounce of energy I spent returned great reward for all of us. Our family learned to be a family who could count on one another. The fun times prepared us for the times to come that would not be so fun.

Linda and I did what we could to be deliberate parents, encouraging teamwork and camaraderie and taking care to give the boys a good spiritual foundation. We continually asked God for help in rearing young men to walk humbly with Him.

At the same time, we knew that we needed to make our marriage relationship a priority. Every now and again, we hired a babysitter for the boys or invited one of their grandmothers over. Then Linda and I got ourselves gussied up for a night out, just the two of us. We often lingered in conversation over a nice dinner before taking in a movie or simply sitting in the park.

One night when I got home from work, Linda met me at the door with a request that made me weak in the knees. "Honey, I want to have an affair." I started to step back. She pulled me in. "With you, Ray," she whispered.

I had no idea a blessed alliance could be so sweet. So strong. So secure. Within the hour, I had picked up a babysitter for the boys and whisked Linda out the door for an overnight date. Keeping our love alive would prove essential to the longstanding survival of our family.

Linda and I treasured every second we could get together, but not to the exclusion of our boys. We treasured every minute we had together with them too! From the time the boys were little, we took them everywhere we went. Christian conferences in the mountains, vacations at the beach, and so much more. We made every trip an adventure!

Once while at a conference in North Carolina, we went to see Blowing Rock and took a train ride with the Tweetsie Railroad through a small mountain pass. The boys were enjoying the time of their lives, pretending to be on a secret mission as steam poured in the open windows. Linda and I settled in to soak up the passing scenery, when suddenly, the train came screeching to a halt. We looked at each other in disbelief, unsure if we should be scared. After a bunch of ruckus, we heard a woman scream. Then more ruckus as strange men appeared at the front of the rail car, wearing bandanas to cover their faces. Wielding guns the size of Texas, they began shouting, "Stay calm! Do as we tell you, and nobody gets hurt." The whole scene, though staged, unnerved every one of us.

AN ESTABLISHED HOME FRONT

The bandits demanded, "Give up your gold!" One of the masked men asked, "Well, whadaya waitin' for, old man?" as he stuck his pistol into the side of a gray-haired gentleman sitting toward the front. The older man resisted, pushing the pistol away with one hand and reaching for the guy's throat with the other.

Scott gasped. "Dad, don't let him do that!"

Adam, being the strong, protective type, hid behind his mom. He reached out for her hand, saying, "It's gonna be okay, Mom. Right?"

Linda looked at me with that playful glint in her eye. "Well, son, I certainly hope so. We have a movie to watch tonight."

Have I mentioned that I love my wife?

Several loud *pops!* jostled every one of us from our seats as another gentleman entered the car from the side door next to where we sat. Smoke curled from the tip of his six-shooter as he twirled it backward and nestled it into the holster on his hip.

The law. He had a long arm and very good aim. The bandits each went down with a thud, grabbing at their chests in desperation.

"Bandit Jesse, you've seen your last ride," the sheriff proclaimed as he stepped toward the front of the car. A cheer went up from every passenger on the train that day, followed by thunderous applause in honor of the lawman who saved the day and a nervous release of laughter.

My boys were so thrilled with the production of the train robbery that they wanted to go back through the pass—after stopping in the gift shop for six-shooters of their own!

We declined the return trip and headed back toward our hotel. It had been a long day filled with great adventure. Definitely one to go down in the Sturt family book of most amazing vacation outings ever.

During our family prayer time before bed that night, we had opportunity to talk about the events of the day. My sons were stricken with the desire to be heroes. Like the lawman, they wanted to be protectors, helping people who had a hard time helping themselves. "Like you, Dad. Just like you."

Stopped me mid sentence, Linda reached over and took my hand in hers, much like the night I gave my life to Christ. Me. Ray Sturt. A hero. I could think of nothing better in the universe than to be the hero of these two fine young boys. I prayed right then and there, *Lord, make me worthy of these deputies. Help us all to be heroes who look to You for help and carry compassion for the lost and those in need of a hand.*

Linda tucked the boys into bed while I excused myself to the other bedroom in the suite. I sat down on the bed, put my head in my hands, and wept. Humble tears. Thankful tears. How did boys like that come to belong to a man like me?

When they were babies, I sometimes wondered whether I would ever be able to influence them for good. Given my history growing up, I worried that I might hide when things got hard, leaving the boys and their mom to figure things out on their own. So far, it seemed I was doing OK. But I certainly was glad I didn't have to do it on my own. Between Linda and me, we provided what our boys needed. The Lord had equipped us, as individuals and as a unit.

Summers with the Sturts filled out nicely with generous amounts of time at Lake Gaston at my parents' lake house. Both Scott and Adam would have gone every single weekend if we could possibly have managed. I guess they took after their mom and me with their love for the outdoors. They swam like fish and used to tease their Grandma Sturt until she came running from the house wearing her old belt float. She would take aim mid run and leap from the dock, shouting, "Whooopeeeeee!" as she landed right in the middle of where the boys were swimming. Splashing and flailing ensued, followed by hearty laughter that bounced from wake to wake across the lake. The sound of their shared laughter still rings in my ears and brings the warmth of a smile to my face.

My mom loved those boys. Dearly loved them. I guess sharing laughter like that was an easier way for her to express her love than to say it out loud. Not so different from when I was a kid. It's what my mom did. She always tried to make things fun for us, even when they weren't. In spite of the difficulty of my childhood, I was glad the boys got to know her and appreciate the lighter side of who she was.

Next to watching my boys splashing around the lake with my mom, skiing was my favorite Lake Gaston activity. As in earlier times, Linda drove the boat while I attempted to stay up on my skis in spite of her shenanigans. The boys didn't really enjoy the challenges of skiing, though they did enjoy being pulled behind the boat on our tow board. And they loved riding in the boat to distract me, squealing with delight when their mom successfully dumped me into the lake.

To get back at them, I filled up squirt bottles, climbed onto my raft, and chased them around the cove. "Take that!" I hollered, unloading my wet friendly fire all over them. Of course, the boys had their own rafts and water bottles, but they let me think I was getting the best of them. Even our miniature dachshund, Prinz Charles Von Sturt, got into the water act, swimming from raft to raft, barking and barking and barking as he tried to catch the squirts before they landed in the lake.

Linda enjoyed lounging lakeside, watching all her crazy boys splashing around in the water. Sometimes she came with me to the other side of the cove in a little two-seater inflatable boat. I rowed while she leaned back against the edge, smiling and singing, happy as a lark.

These were stolen moments of inexplicable joy. Moments that I would one day strain to remember. If I had known how hard it would be to bring them back, I would have taken more care to seal them as they happened.

As Scott and Adam got older, our times at the lake expanded into high-risk adventures. We packed our guns! I had a 12-gauge Fox double-barreled shotgun, and the boys each had a BB gun. I mean to tell you, Linda nearly suffered a dozen heart attacks every weekend! Though she would say that every one of them was worth seeing her boys take down milk jugs, soda cans, and an occasional snake.

One afternoon while she sunned herself on the pier with her back to me, I snuck in tight to the shoreline for a look at something slinking through the water. *BOOM!* Missed. A water snake. *BOOM!* Got him! And I got Linda too! Water sprayed all the way up and over her chair.

"Why didn't you warn me? Give me that gun!" she bellowed, scrambling to get out of her chair. Linda couldn't stay angry with me for long. She always had that special glint in her eye. When she turned toward me, the late summer sun caught her face just right. For an instant, she practically glowed. Just like an angel. My angel.

Our family spent many seasons at the lake house. One season we watched the boys pile their stuffed animals into a wheelbarrow as they helped us haul the raked-up leaves. The next they were running around swinging their Easter baskets, looking for dyed eggs as well as colorful plastic ones filled with money.

Easters hold a special place in the Sturt household. After church, we enjoyed a special dinner with Grandpa and Grandma Glass. Then we took off for Lake Gaston to celebrate with Grandma and Grandpa Sturt.

Grandma Sturt's lamb cakes were always a highlight! Every year she made one for Scott and Adam, covered in sweet white frosting and coconut with raisins set in place for the eyes and nose. She tied a tiny bell around its neck with red ribbon and surrounded it on a tray with marshmallow peeps, candy eggs, and jelly beans. Then she set it on display as a touch point for my boys to hear the Easter story.

And what a story. Our Lord, Jesus, the sacrificial Lamb, risen from death to take His place on heaven's throne. Every year, along with taking a picture of the boys with their grandma's lamb cake, we read John 1:29 as a family from our old King James Bible: "Behold, the Lamb of God, which taketh away the sin of the world." So profound, to gain life from death. If Linda and I could give our boys one thing, it would be the grounding of their lives in the truth of their living Lord.

AN ESTABLISHED HOME FRONT

Looking back, this gift of life gave our family such promise when we were young and finding our way. Hear me: the mercy of the Lord shone down all around us. There is no way, given the life I experienced as a child, that I would ever imagine a Father who loved without limits. Who believed without proof. Who equipped for victory without expectation of payment in return. But here we were. I believe the Lord was strengthening us for battles to come.

Linda and I believed in doing everything we could to build a solid foundation for our family. So we decided to purchase a time-share week in a condo on Virginia Beach, close to home and just for us. We packed our bags every June for a week away. The first request when we reached the sand? "Daddy, dig us a hole!"

It threatened to take me back to a day when holes were snares, designed for capture. I fell prey to a few of those throughout my young life. I desired for my boys something better. So every year, I dug for them a hole. A hole in which they would discover the gift of laughter, not a trap. It would serve as a means through which laughter not only came but multiplied. A life-sustaining gift. A gift to strengthen our homefront, not take away its life.

Linda and I recognized that giving our boys these gifts would help them in whatever battles were to come. Battles that loomed, unaware to us, just around the corner.

CHAPTER 5

ENCROACHMENT

For our struggle is not against flesh and blood, but against the rulers, against the authorities, against the powers of this dark world and against the spiritual forces of evil in the heavenly realms.
—Ephesians 6:12

I loved spending time with my boys. They were the world to me. At every opportunity, we made fish sticks and French fries before hitting the living room for "wrestle mania." On a warm August evening in 1987, though, extreme pains in my upper abdomen prevented the wrestling. After dinner, I lay down on the floor and begged the boys to jump up and down on my stomach. Literally. They obliged, though they didn't comprehend the immensity of the situation. After a while, I stopped hurting and engaged in our normal manic activity.

A few weeks later, we packed for our week in the condo at Virginia Beach. Along the way, we stopped for burgers and fries. I gobbled my food and immediately experienced regret. As soon as the tastiness hit my stomach, I began to writhe in pain. I remembered that fast food had triggered a similar response a couple of weeks back. I broke out in a sweat, and Linda had to drive the rest of the way to the beach.

Upon our arrival, the boys helped Linda unload the car, and I went straight for bed, wishing I knew why my body seemed to be rebelling against the food I liked the most. Was there anything I could eat without these awful side effects?

When Linda came to bed, she checked me over and asked me a lot of questions. As my wife, and with her experience as a registered nurse, I trusted her suggestions without wavering an iota. She speculated that my gallbladder might be acting up.

Gallbladder attacks? Was that all? Well, that could be managed easily. All I had to do was wait out our vacation, watch what I ate, and head straight for the doctor when we got back. No problem.

As suspected, the doctor ordered an upper-gastro X-ray. But the X-ray indicated an unexpected result: duodenitis, an inflammation in the first part of the intestine, just to the side of my stomach. The doctor prescribed Pepcid and sent me on my way. But the pain continued, every day, even though I took the medication twice a day.

When I discovered that I ran a low-grade fever in the afternoons, I returned to my family doctor for a referral to a gastroenterologist. He performed a scope and ran a large battery of tests, looking for the possibility of parasites or bacteria. Nothing. He found nothing that would account for the extreme pain and constant fever. After diagnosing me with inflammation of the esophagus and stomach, he advised that I reduce the stress in my life. I couldn't believe my ears. Linda and the boys had already picked up on many of my duties around the house, including cutting the grass. To have any less stress, I would have to be lying in bed 24/7!

Hearing what the doctor ordered, and knowing that Linda felt sure I had gallbladder disease, I took the medicine and promptly returned to work. If I could better manage my diet and begin to pinpoint the cause of the pains on my own, maybe I could help the doctors help me. Within weeks, I experienced a spell of extreme pains shooting across my upper abdomen. My family doctor drew blood and informed me that I had pancreatitis. *Fine*, I thought. *I'll add that to the list.* Gastritis, esophagitis, duodenitis, and pancreatitis.

ENCROACHMENT

I took the medicine and stayed home from work, lying on the deck and resting in the sunshine. When I returned to the doctor for a follow-up visit, he accused me of being a drinker. Stupified, I assured him that I did *not* drink or smoke and I was trying to follow a healthy diet, but nothing seemed to be working.

Finally, hearing my complaints, the doctor admitted me into a surgeon's care at the hospital in Hopewell, five miles from our home. Built on a cliff overlooking the beautiful Appomattox River, the setting of this hospital put many at ease, helping them to feel peaceful despite their illnesses. I felt anything but peaceful. I wondered whether this could be the beginning of the end of my life. I began to pray. *Lord, please don't take my boys' father from them. They're too young. They need me, and I need You.*

Within hours, the doctor ordered an ultrasound on my gallbladder. Finally, someone who made sense! "Thank you!" I said, after the specialist marked my chart.

While Linda and I awaited the results of the procedure, we discussed the possibilities of surgery. Who would watch the boys? How many days might I need off work for recovery time? As a plan began to emerge, the doctor came into the room with surprising news. He could find nothing wrong with my gallbladder. The ultrasound showed a completely healthy organ. Every test came back negative.

And every attack took more and more away from a productive, healthy lifestyle. My family began to feel the effects of being thrust into this emerging new battleground. Anger began to seep into everyday conversations. I could no longer romp with the boys or make them my gourmet meals or take them to the lake for target practice.

Some days this illness felt an awful lot like punishment, for them and for me. My heart ached. I cried out in the silence of my room. *Lord, have mercy. I submit to You the rest of my days. Please, Lord, reveal to the doctors the root of these issues and return to me my life.*

The doctors checked everything they could think of. Though I had no issues with my heart other than the longing to be well, they did an echocardiogram. Everything showed up normal; the test found no endocarditis.

Hope for recovery sank with each passing day as well-meaning friends inundated me with home remedies.

"Try some herbs, Ray."

"Get more rest, Ray."

"De-stress your life, Ray."

"Stay away from the dog, Ray."

Pardon me? Yes, sir, that's what he said. My father, believing he could manage the universe if it gave him half a chance, determined that Charlie must have contracted some sort of crazy illness that he, in turn, passed on to me. Charlie, our well-vaccinated dachshund? The only thing Charlie contracted was loneliness.

"Please get better soon, Ray." Linda. My Linda. Her tone, filled with compassion, revealed her exhaustion. "Life at home isn't the same without you. School keeps the boys occupied, though they ask me every day when you'll be home. Even Charlie's sad. We're all sad."

No one escaped the ripple effects of this siege against my body.

After five days in the hospital, the surgeon sent me home with two prescriptions, an antibiotic and an antifungal drug. "One of these two ought to kill what's ailin' you," the surgeon declared.

My family doctor responded with, "He's covering you both ways, Ray."

Linda didn't think the drugs would cover me at all.

She was right. Two weeks after my discharge from the hospital, a high fever landed me back at the surgeon's office. He stood shaking his head in disbelief, while I sat on the table, my head hung in sheer exhaustion. I wasn't ready to hear his recommendation. "Go back to the gastro, Ray."

More prodding. More tests. More negative results.

Weeks and months passed without letup from the pain. I kept trying to return to work in an attempt to get on with my life, but another attack interrupted every return. Missing work like to have killed me. I loved creating metal parts and repairing broken ones.

ENCROACHMENT

A couple of my doctors thought I might just be trying to get out of work. Me. Ray Sturt. Recipient of the Perfect Attendance Award from Prince George High School. And if one more doctor poked my abdomen and then just shook his head at me, I thought I might kick him in the nose! Doctors really should pay attention to where they're standing when they start poking on sensitive parts.

And doctors really should pay attention to the complaints of their patients and observe their symptoms with keen awareness. Because the machines couldn't prove that I was sick, the doctors believed I must not be.

But I was telling the truth. No matter what the machines were saying.

After the doctors came up empty-handed for three months, a friend of Linda's connected me with her gastroenterologist in Richmond. I sure was tired of making these trips to the doctor. Every new option brought me a glimmer of hope for a diagnosis and solution. But with every new option that became a closed door, the light of hope became weaker and weaker. Without Linda advocating for me, I'm sure I would have given up. Sure of it.

On a morning in late November, Linda packed up my medical records and loaded them with me in the car for the drive to Richmond.

My Linda. So tired. So filled with determination. Still so in love. Really, truly in love. The kind of love that most of us never find, and once we find it, we surely don't deserve it. I leaned over and took her hand from the steering wheel before we backed out of the driveway that morning. Right then and there, I offered to the Lord a prayer of thanksgiving for my beloved bride. Oh, how grateful I was that He had given her to be my partner, my ally, my friend.

After a quick visit in his office, this new doctor nodded. I held my breath. Then he advised that I check into the hospital in Richmond right away for further testing and observation. I let out my breath. This was not a relief, but maybe he would see something that no one else had seen. Optimism was fading from my vocabulary.

I went. And over the course of the next week, testing happened. Many were repeats, but new tests were ordered too. They did a HIDA scan and a CAT scan, injecting me with dye and taking X-rays with me in positions I didn't know I could get into. Consulting doctors buzzed through my room every hour of the day—an infectious disease specialist, a surgeon, a psychiatrist. More prodding. More speculating. Then the whispering.

Finally the psychiatrist decided to probe further. He set an appointment to see Linda in the middle of the day. She didn't want to have to rush, so she talked my parents into staying with Scott and Adam.

My father dragged his feet as usual. "There's nothing wrong with Ray. Just bring him home," he said. He hadn't heard or understood me my whole life. I shouldn't have expected that he might start now. At least he and Mom agreed to help Linda with the boys, even if she did have to twist their arms. If not for being so sick, I might have felt a little more grateful.

The doctor came to spend time with me before seeing Linda and me together. He asked us both a lot of questions to help him with a diagnosis and treatment plan. We soon found out that he had no plan at all. The consensus of all the research and tests? I wasn't really sick.

The awkward silence of this disease—whatever it was—stifled me. And it baffled the professionals.

I so wished that I could take it by the hand, walk right up to each one of the doctors and formally introduce them, just as my dad had done with my teacher when I was in the third grade. What do you mean you haven't seen Ray all day? Madam, he's right here. Right where he's been all along. Sir, you can't see this disease? Well, it and I are well acquainted. I can assure you, it is alive and present. Right where it's been all along. Here. Let me introduce you.

Being invisible no longer suited me. I found my voice, used it well, and still, nobody heard me. If I could have gone straight for the door, I would have. But I had to wait for my inevitable release.

ENCROACHMENT

It came. And I went back home, ever more aware of the battle for my life. I could feel the enemy pressing in. Pushing me back. Threatening. Lurking.

I refused to surrender. I wanted my life back. My work. My family. My freedom.

With my ally beside me, I attempted once more to fight back. Live my life. I tried to reengage with the boys. For Halloween that year, they dressed up as Sting and the Ax Man. Shrieks of terror echoed throughout the neighborhood as small children came into contact with the scary look those boys managed. Amazing what a little face paint will do.

I also began going back to church whenever possible, and I returned to work. In spite of the pain. In spite of the fever. But the enemy snagged me with the same old snare. I couldn't go around it. I couldn't keep food in my system. I was done.

In short order, I returned to Richmond to see the stomach specialist as an outpatient. Another CAT scan. Again, negative. Then the doctor recommended something that hadn't been done before, an ERCP. It involved swallowing a snaking tube with a light on it, which wasn't pleasant. But to tell the truth, I would have swallowed a live snake, at that point, if it offered me the hope of a diagnosis and an end to the pain. The test also involved shooting dye directly into the bile duct going into the gallbladder, as well as into the pancreatic duct. It allowed the doctor to see what couldn't otherwise be seen on an X-ray or CAT scan.

Upon completion of the procedure, the doctor consulted with Linda. "The results were inconclusive," he said without blinking. "We couldn't visualize the common duct at all. The dye simply did not go into the gallbladder."

Linda told me about the doctor's report once the twilight medication wore off at home. Every nerve in my body seemed to explode with the news. It must have been evident to Linda that I was about to leap out of bed in anger. She gently slipped her hand in mine. Like a tiny rudder steering a ship in a raging storm, that single act of love and connection from Linda guided me into safer waters, calming me right down.

"We have heard the same conclusions from every medical professional who opened my chart over the past four months," I said. "Something is wrong, Linda. Terribly wrong."

My quality of life deteriorated to the point that I could no longer shoot a BB gun with my boys or treat my beloved wife to a nice evening out or minister to the kids in the neighborhood. I couldn't even effectively perform the tasks necessary to make machine parts, the job that I'd known and loved my entire life. Linda, with the help of the boys, mowed the grass, cooked our meals, cleaned the house, and raked the leaves while I sat.

I sat, and I waited. I sat, and I waited, and I sat some more. How would those doctors feel to watch life go on around them while they sat at the mercy of the pain?

Silence lingered for what seemed a lifetime.

Finally, Linda interrupted the awkward pause. Our eyes met as she held back tears. "I know, Ray. I know how you feel. Why won't they listen to us? Why do we have to settle for their generic response? 'There's nothing more we can do.' They say they're sorry, but I don't believe them anymore." A tear dripped from Linda's face as she slipped her arm under mine. My wife is the most amazing woman on the face of the earth.

"I love you," I whispered, following the trail of the tear with the tip of my finger.

I felt Linda's love and support every time she explained my symptoms to another doctor. Using her more-than-nineteen-years' experience in the medical profession, Linda had exhausted herself gathering information, recording observations, and advocating on my behalf with the doctors. She could do nothing more to help the doctors opt for surgery based on their observation and intuition as well as her own. It seemed obvious that only gallbladder disease could cause all the related issues with which I had been diagnosed: gastritis, esophagitis, duodenitis, and pancreatitis.

Helpless to do anything else, she did the one thing left she knew to do. She prayed. Fervently, unswervingly, submitting the entire situation for the first time to the holy and complete will of God.

Of course we had prayed throughout this whole process, for the doctors, for the medicine to work. And Lord knows we prayed for healing. But now Linda looked only to God on my behalf because I was nearing the edge of done.

God, You are the giver of life. In you we live and move and have our being. I submit to you my worry. My striving. My Ray. He is yours. It seems that the enemy has surrounded us. Please, God, show us what to do next. We don't have a clue. But we know You do. So, we trust You for Your plan. For Your timing. Amen.

Every day Linda prayed that prayer. She would tell you that some version of this prayer was on her mind every minute of the day. *Show us, God. Please. Show us.*

Word of these months of struggle reached into our community. The doctors' proclamations that they couldn't find anything wrong with me caused even our close friends to question the validity of my pain. That hurt me. It especially hurt me that they didn't offer Linda the support she needed while she poured herself into helping me. I suppose people just didn't know what to think or how to help. So they did nothing, but Linda could have used a few friends to take her to lunch or a movie sometimes.

We became less and less affected by the pain inflicted by others, even when they meant well. We were learning to rely more and more on God. As long as we had each other and we had Him to lean on, the enemy could surround us with ten thousand men, and we would not fear.

In the meantime, waiting on what God would have us do, our family doctor popped in on Linda during one of her shifts at the hospital. "How's Ray?" he asked.

"Well, doctor, Ray's getting along the best he can. He's still carrying a fever every day, and he's in an awful lot of pain."

The doctor inquired further, asking how the ERCP test had gone during our last visit to Richmond. Linda explained that the test had been inconclusive because they couldn't get the dye into the gallbladder at all.

"Linda, that's not normal. Dye always goes into the gallbladder. There must be some sort of blockage there, somewhere. Let's get Ray set up for an exploratory." In short order, our family physician gave us a referral to another surgeon in Hopewell.

Christmas came calling a little early for the Sturts in 1987. On December 16, I finally had my gallbladder removed! When I woke up from the anesthesia, the pain was gone. Gone! Hallelujah! Me. Ray Sturt. Pain free. What do you think about that? I like to have cried. As a little extra gift for the holidays, the surgeon left behind a nice-looking five-inch incision, angled just under my right rib cage. I decided I could live with that for a few days after all I been through. Noooo problem!

It had taken the new surgeon a little time to go through my stack of records, three inches thick. But in the end, he determined that the exploratory laparotomy was indeed the way to go. It allowed him to check for tumors or other defects, including adhesions from my childhood appendectomy. He agreed to remove my gallbladder even if he didn't see evidence of disease when he went in.

I mean to tell you, I was happy he did! The pathology report confirmed that the tissues of the gallbladder showed mononuclear cells growing in the wall of the gallbladder, causing it to thicken. Final diagnosis? Chronic cholecystitis! How sweet to read those words in black-and-white.

"Linda! Can you believe it?" Proof of my illness had been hiding in the tissues of the gallbladder all along. While I didn't understand a single thing about why, I knew the Lord who did. Linda helped me to trust God more, even when I didn't see His plan. It's harder when you're in the middle of a trial to remember you don't have to know it all. I was so glad to see that suffering come to an end.

Though it may have only paved the way for a deeper experience with suffering than I could have imagined.

After seeing ten doctors and my insurance company paying out eighteen thousand dollars in addition to our deductibles, I received one simple gallbladder surgery, a surgery that would have cost only four thousand dollars if it had been completed when the symptoms first began. And it would not have stolen five months of my life.

But it wouldn't be long until our family would begin to see a toll far greater than any amount of cash.

A complex puzzle, complicated by the fact that the medical community considered gallbladder disease to be something contracted by the "fair, fat, and forty," my case astounded every doctor, it seemed, in a fifty-mile radius. While I had turned forty that year, my body didn't match up with my chronological age. Daily crunches, weight lifting, and a regimen of exercises kept me in great physical shape. My gallbladder had no stones, no sludge, no crystals. It's no wonder, really, that the disease was difficult to diagnose in me.

But for me the difficulty opened the door to many questions. During the ordeal, I was reminded often of my childhood when no one would listen to me. When I did speak up or show that I was in pain, my dad turned away in disbelief, just as he had done at the hospital years before.

I suppose some of my questions after my surgery were similar to those I asked as a child, most of them starting with *why*. Why was I on earth? Why did I have to be sick, Lord? Why did I have such a rare gallbladder disease? Was it a punishment? Sometimes as a kid I considered my isolation and hiddenness a punishment. Did I need to be taught a lesson? Had I learned it, or would there be more? Should I feel guilty for something I did or didn't do that brought on this correction?

Was it a test of faith? I knew that trials helped to grow faith. First Peter 1:6–7 says, "In this you greatly rejoice, though now for a little while you may have had to suffer grief in all kinds of trials. These have come so that your faith—of greater worth than gold, which perishes even though refined by fire—may be proved genuine and may result in praise, glory and honor when Jesus Christ is revealed." I had been a faithful, and I mean faithful, servant of the Lord for fifteen years. I didn't understand.

And I wondered where all my faithful, believing friends had gone. I heard through Linda that they were praying, but I didn't see any of them stepping in alongside me to fight or offer good biblical counsel. I needed a spiritual perspective. I needed someone to point me toward Scripture. To hold me up.

Silence.

I was in crisis.

And in the silence, I dug myself deep into depression. Confusion, frustration, and discouragement took over my thinking. Anger filled up my spirit. It had begun during the time of waiting and intensified in the quiet of recovery. I walked a couple of miles every day so I could regain my strength. But six weeks was a long time to be off work.

Each night after school, the boys begged me to pull up to the table with them to play a board game, watch *The Dukes of Hazard* on TV, anything. "You get to choose which one!" Adam announced.

"You choose!" I retorted. "I'm not in the mood."

Those boys didn't deserve to be treated like that. They were kind boys, strong and fun. If I would have let them, maybe they could have helped me keep my head up. But they were out of my line of sight. I could only see myself. I watched, helplessly, as I slid from entertaining a hint of thankfulness to carrying a load of bitterness.

Darkness settled in. With the front lines shifting, I could feel the enemy's circle tightening, digging trenches and laying groundwork for the next stage of the battle. His boldness grew. Only now do I recognize his face. "For our struggle is not against flesh and blood, but against the rulers, against the authorities, against the powers of this dark world and against the spiritual forces of evil in the heavenly realms" (Eph. 6:12).

I withdrew.

In my vulnerability, the enemy wore me down. Pushed me back. He blocked my life supply, and I stepped out onto the slippery path that marred my fellowship with God and hindered communion with my wife.

BIPOLAR VICTORY

Our Wedding Day! Thanksgiving, November 23, 1972

ENCROACHMENT

Digging a hole in the sand at Virginia Beach

Ray, Scott and Adam at Lake Gaston

BIPOLAR VICTORY

Grandma Sturt's lamb cake baked every Easter for Scott & Adam

Here we are at Tweetsie Railroad

ENCROACHMENT

Ray and Charlie at Lake Gaston

Scott, Adam & Charlie Dog with rafts on Lake Gaston

BIPOLAR VICTORY

Scott, Ray and Sophie at our tri-level house after Scott's hand accident

Ray wearing his Bipolar Victory cap and jacket 2005

ENCROACHMENT

The Bipolar Victory cap and jacket

Ray smiling at one of his garden plots in our former backyard 2005

BIPOLAR VICTORY

Linda picking string beans by the bucket from another garden plot in 2005

Adam over looking the Shenandoah River

72

ENCROACHMENT

Adam playing his Gibson ES-175

Scott with his viola and the hand bow attachment in 2006.

CHAPTER 6

RULES OF ENGAGEMENT

*Trust in the LORD with all thine heart;
and lean not unto thine own understanding.
In all thy ways acknowledge him, and he shall direct thy paths.*
—Proverbs 3:5–6 KJV

From Linda

When I met Ray for the first time, my heart skipped a beat. His tall stature and blazing blue eyes caught my attention. He carried a head full of dark blond hair and a stunning smile. He seemed outgoing and kept his tone friendly. His rolled-up sleeves gave away his physical strength. But a man who would stand in his father's hospital room so his mother wouldn't have to be there alone revealed a different kind of strength altogether.

I had been on the lookout for a man of strong character and gentleness of heart, someone I could respect and who wanted to share life together. I didn't know I would find him leaning against the wall in one of my patients' rooms! It just goes to show how creative the Lord can be with introductions.

While I needed a bit of a nudge to commit to life with this man, I can't imagine life with anyone else. Ray and I seemed perfectly compatible and extremely comfortable with each other from the minute he showed up at my door for our first date. I noticed right away that Ray paid attention. He had lots to say, but he listened intently when it was my turn to talk. Our conversations could have gone straight into the next day if we had let them. I had never met a man with such passion and conviction. We saw eye to eye on so many things, right from the start. And we shared more common interests than I ever thought possible. The outdoors, sports, and even serving at church.

Imagine my delight when Ray and I set a date for our wedding—Thanksgiving Day! A day of thanks to remember that God brought us together. At first, we intended just to exchange wedding bands. But when Ray asked what I wanted for my birthday, I said that I would like an engagement ring.

We did everything together, so we headed off as a couple to the jewelry store—Ray with his pocket full of cash and me with my inexpensive tastes. I was so excited for our special day that I barely heard the clerk tell us about all the different rings.

Without the fanfare of drumrolls or twinkling stars, Ray slipped a diamond ring on my finger. We sat quietly in his baby blue LTD. The glimmer of the sunshine filled the air around us, dancing on the diamond and bringing joy to my heart. I had found my knight in shining armor.

"Thank you," I whispered, as we sealed the deal with a kiss.

With our commitment, God opened for us a piece of heaven on earth. The alliance He intended solidified quickly. Even when, after our wedding, challenges came that we didn't quite expect. We moved into the mobile home that Ray owned at his parents' park. While I anticipated a few issues with settling in so close to his parents, I didn't recognize them as spies. Yes! They spied on us! Every move we made came under the watchful eyes of Alice and Joe. They disapproved of a lot of things we did, like going to the launderette and planting marigolds alongside the patio.

RULES OF ENGAGEMENT

Sweet Ray. He couldn't speak ill against his parents. "They mean well," he'd say. But I knew better. They just couldn't stand that their son had his own life with a wife to care for and soon a baby on the way! Still, in order to keep peace, I went along with as many of their demands as I could. I actually didn't mind eating meals with them on occasion. Sometimes Alice had meals ready so that when Ray and I got home from work, all we had to do was sit down and eat. Yes, I do think she meant well. But when she scolded us for buying a dryer when Scott was born, that seemed a little too far over the edge. I had a newborn baby to care for, who required many diaper changes every single day and went through at least three outfits in a twenty-four-hour period. I needed to be able to take care of our laundry needs without lugging everything up to the house.

Our stint at Hilltop Trailer Park lasted approximately eighteen months. It turned out to be a just-right adjustment time for all of us.

I was glad that we got to land there for a while. I think Ray was too. Some others in the park were, as well, especially the military doctor who lived in the very front lot. One morning, as we saw him getting into his car, he said, "What happened? Did the water pump blow up? I haven't had but a trickle in my shower the whole time I've lived here, until today."

Well, all we had was a trickle at first too. But then Ray remembered that he and his dad had combined pipes for the two pumps connected with the house and cut off one of the in-line valves. He went straight to the valve, opened it up, and we never had a trickling shower again. Neither did the families in any of the other twelve trailers whose intake was on that valve. That's my Ray. So gifted and so aware.

We got a good laugh out of that one. I don't know if Ray's dad ever realized that Ray had opened up the valve to give tenants full water pressure. He wouldn't have been happy. But I was proud of Ray for doing what was right.

My Ray. He always had other people in mind. Always. Even when he wasn't quite himself. After his gallbladder surgery, the days when he was himself were farther and farther between.

"Linda," Ray announced one morning, standing square in our bedroom doorway. "I think we should get a divorce and split up the estate."

His words about knocked my knees out from under me. Split the estate? What about splitting me straight through the heart? I couldn't believe my ears. I had dedicated my life to this man. I loved him. I really did love him. I couldn't imagine being without him. I took a second to catch my breath, whispering a desperate plea for the Lord to help.

"Ray Sturt, eighteen years ago I vowed to stay with you until one of us died. As far as I can tell, we are both still breathing."

But the truth was that Ray's "breathing" had become more and more labored since his surgery. The struggle to find the source of his illness and get it taken care of really took a toll on his emotional well-being. It had taken a toll on both of us. We were exhausted. It had been a hard fall and an even harder winter.

In the middle of it all, Christmas came, though we experienced very little of the merry side of the holiday. We tried to make it good for the boys, decorating some at home and exchanging a few presents. But my mother-in-law, who didn't believe that Ray really was sick, got things started when she surprised Ray with a decorated Christmas tree for his hospital room. I think she may have been apologizing, though she would never say that out loud.

After plugging in the lights and tweaking a few of the dangling bulbs, she stood back to admire her presentation. "Why, lookie there, Ray, you have your own little Christmas tree. Do you like it?" she prodded.

He nodded, but it was hard to know whether he truly liked it. He didn't respond well to visitors after his surgery. He was distant with his mom and sometimes even with me. It pained me deeply to watch him become so despondent. I felt helpless.

RULES OF ENGAGEMENT

I wanted Ray back. My Ray. The Ray who sat up with me when the boys were babies because he loved being with us. The Ray who protected me from snakes and other sorts of varmints, even when I didn't need protecting. The Ray who went through life with a gleam in his eye and a passion for people. He worked hard. He loved well. He lived every minute to its fullest. Oh, how I missed him.

The boys missed him too. When Ray first started feeling sick, he still took us down to the park on weekends to walk the trails and toss a football with the boys. Our Charlie bounced along with us like he owned the place. Ray hurt, but he wouldn't have passed up that time with us for the world.

After Ray's surgery, everything changed. He still helped to take Adam for his piano and tennis lessons. We both ran Scott to his viola lessons. We continued our beach-week vacation and weekends at the lake. But Ray didn't engage like he used to. He was present, but distant. He didn't shoot with the boys or do much skiing. In fact, he rarely ventured far from the condo except for an occasional stroll along the boardwalk.

When he went back to work after the normal six-week recovery, it helped him immensely to get out of the house and feel productive again. But demands were high. He couldn't keep up. Some of his co-workers complained to the boss that he spent too much time in flirtatious fun instead of working. The supervisor got on him about it. This wasn't my Ray.

Some of our friends at church noticed that he wasn't himself. His passion for people still drove his decisions, so he agreed to take a class called Evangelism Explosion. He wanted with all of his heart to effectively share the gospel with the lost. This class reconnected him with that passion and got him back into fellowship with people at church. I was thrilled about his interest and prayed that it might be something to draw him back toward being himself. But the class was hard. He came home frustrated every week. It involved a lot of memorization and verbal exercises in small groups. In an instant, it overwhelmed him. He became easily confused, and he couldn't get the words out of his mouth. Some of his classmates became irritated, thinking he was refusing to participate. My heart sank.

Months went by with this pattern of attempts and failures. He tried hard to take back the life he knew and desired, but it denied him access. I couldn't understand it. Eventually he gave up. He stopped going to church. He even stopped worrying about his performance at work. This wasn't my Ray.

I tried not to panic. Ray needed me not to panic. So I did what I knew to do. I prayed. *Please, God, bring Ray back around to health. Help him to be present and active in our life together. I miss him. Desperately. My life isn't the same without him in it.*

Ray continued to withdraw. Some weeks, his spiraling seemed to accelerate at such a high rate that I hardly recognized him in the blur. I had been a registered nurse for many years and could have managed a number of illnesses from a practical, one-day-at-a-time approach. It's hard to imagine that cancer would have been preferable to this, or even a heart attack, but it's true. A mental disorder stretched the boundaries of manageability for me. I had no expertise. I had no support. I was mortified by the possible stigma staring us in the face.

At first, I kept quiet about Ray's deteriorating condition. I decided for myself that he was experiencing a midlife crisis, and I determined to manage it on my own. I would just need to be a kinder, more-patient and more-appealing wife to bridge the gap for him during this time of transition.

I bought fancy nightgowns and lotions, booked getaways, always looked my best, and cooked his best meals. Nothing seemed to connect. He fidgeted and fussed, even during meals. He constantly rearranged his utensils and was never satisfied with their placement. Every few minutes he would lift his plate and bend over to look under it with a scowl the size of Texas.

Secrecy and suspicion seemed to occupy his thoughts. One evening after working the evening shift at the hospital, I came home around midnight to complete darkness. The garage door wouldn't open, and I couldn't find my keys. I stood on the porch fumbling in the dark for more than ten minutes before I actually made it into the house. Every light was off. I'm sure it was deliberate. Ray sent a clear message that night. I wasn't wanted. But he didn't have a choice.

I quietly changed my clothes and slipped into bed beside this man I hardly recognized. I had promised to be his ally until separated by death. Ray stirred. Holding on as tightly as I could to the remnant of respect I still had for my husband, I braced myself for his response. He flung a string of ugliness over his shoulder as I settled in. Something about making too much noise. "Don't you know people are trying to #*#*# sleep around here?"

I found out in the morning that Ray had actually turned off the garage-door opener. He didn't want me anymore. It stung like an arrow piercing straight through my heart. We were losing the battle.

Ray's vacillating moods continued to intensify. Rudeness, at times laced with profanity, became his normal way of communicating. I never knew who to expect when he walked in the door. Mr. Pleasant or Mr. Grouchy? Mr. Up or Mr. Down? I walked on eggshells and worked hard to keep peace. If I didn't hold things together, our family would fall apart. Without question, my family was worth everything it would take.

Scott and Adam, both at critical stages of life when they needed their father, seemed to fare better than some might expect through these difficult times. They were both active in school, enjoyed each other's company, and shared the gift of music. They also had their friends, so most everything but their father was stable and supportive. I was so grateful for my friends who pitched in on occasion with rides or to take the boys overnight. It helped me shield my sons from Ray's hurtfulness while also protecting Ray. He often couldn't help his behavior and felt so sorry afterward.

After a particularly rough few days, when the eggshells seemed to be cutting straight through the skin, Ray came to where I was working in the spare room downstairs. His face wet with tears, he dropped to his knees at my feet and wrapped his arms around my legs. Here was my strong, capable Ray, reduced to a puddle of remorse.

Between sobs, with words barely recognizable, he pleaded, "Please forgive me. I'm so sorry for what I put you through. I'm not worthy of your love. But I can't live without it." Ray clung to me like a child just waking up from a horrific nightmare.

We huddled together that night for what seemed like hours. Clinging. Crying. Caught in the middle of something neither of us could see.

Though Ray received treatment from our family doctor, as well as from a local psychiatrist, the stability of his condition continued to waver. His outbursts became more and more unpredictable.

One afternoon I received a call from Ray's supervisor. "Linda, I'm calling out of concern for you, for Ray, and for your family. Today Ray got irritated with something one of the guys said. Something flipped in him like a switch on a time bomb. He began to spew forth threats in a way I've never heard before. Your quiet, kind husband got very angry. He threatened to bring a gun and blow us all away if we didn't stop staring and get back to work."

I needed to take action. We were no longer safe. Ray was no longer safe. He needed inpatient psychiatric treatment. My whole being trembled at the thought. Every time I tried to say it out loud, I broke into tears. This would not go well if Ray refused to go, and I suspected he might put up a fuss. There would be no turning back. If he fought, my only alternative would be to have him admitted into a mental facility against his will. *Lord, please. Have mercy.*

Evening came, and I made my move. Ray agreed. He would go to see another psychiatrist in Richmond and allow himself to begin inpatient treatment immediately. Relief flooded through me like a torrent of water released at the peak of a storm.

I made an appointment the next day.

On the morning Ray was to see his new psychiatrist, I came downstairs to find him waiting at the door with his suitcase in hand. My steps grew shorter and slower as I crossed the room toward him. I hated wondering which Ray I would find when I came into a room that he already occupied. He leaned toward me. I stopped. He reached up and gently pushed my hair back from my face. I tried not to turn away. His hand lingered on my cheek. Tears filled his eyes, as he brushed his lips against mine. His tenderness showed what he could not say.

Only tears fell into our silent space. In a sweet act of mercy, the Lord gave us these few minutes together before we got in the car to drive headlong into the hardest season of our married life.

The bleak landscape of February seemed a perfect picture of how I felt when the hospital door closed and locked behind me, leaving my strong, tenderhearted Ray inside. I knew I should feel grateful for so many things. Ray's psychiatrist sent us straight to the hospital after his evaluation, as we had hoped. Ray was ready.

Still, anger and guilt pushed their way to the edge of my restraint, and I broke. *Why did this have to happen to us?* I steadied myself against a pillar to catch my breath. Lies filled my head. Questions of Ray's safety. Wondering whether I had done the right thing. Worry about how I would ever make it through life if Ray didn't recover. What would the boys do without their father's love and influence? The staff assured me that Ray would receive excellent care. I wanted to believe them. I needed to believe them.

After the initial release of the burden of grief, I began to feel a real sense of relief. Relief that I had done the right thing. Relief that I didn't have to be aware of Ray's presence and mood in every corner of the house. It allowed me some quiet time to spend with God. To heal. To pray. To be.

One afternoon, while making rounds on the floor at the hospital, an urgent phone call threatened to bring my quiet to an abrupt halt. My mother was suffering from congestive heart failure. In her eighties and facing open-heart surgery, she was apprehensive, and so was I. How was I going to manage this? Ray and now my mom. Who would watch over my boys? What about work?

"Trust in the LORD with all thine heart; and lean not unto thine own understanding. In all thy ways acknowledge him, and he shall direct thy path" (Prov. 3:5–6 KJV). This passage was among the first I memorized as a child. I hid the Word of the Lord in my heart for such times as these. If I had known how difficult life would become, I would have memorized more verses. *Lord, You are my only hope. My redeemer. My protector. In You, I place my trust. I give to You my Ray, my mom, my sons. See us through this season of challenge. Give me the strength and courage I need for every day. Every hour.*

Every hour I turned to the Lord, my never-out source of strength.

CHAPTER 7

BEHIND ENEMY LINES

We must learn to regard people less in light of what they do or omit to do, and more in the light of what they suffer.
—Dietrich Bonhoeffer

When we arrived at the psychiatric hospital and began walking toward the entrance, every section of the sidewalk came at me one queasy step at a time. I never knew how my brain was going to process an experience. Sometimes it appeared like a frame out of focus, other times as if someone were yanking my film right out of the projector. Today's action was so slow everything seemed to pile up. I couldn't put my finger on which frame held the here and now. I could hear Linda's voice, so I just kept focusing on that.

Eventually, with her help, I began to notice the beautiful parklike setting. Flowerbeds lined the walkway leading to the entrance. Park benches sat scattered around the property. By the time we reached the red brick building I had relaxed a little. Relaxing never came easy.

My thoughts constantly competed for attention. They would either short each other out or get all tangled up together. I truly hoped this place would give me a short break from the chaos, at the very least. But ideally? I needed a new lease on life, a complete makeover.

As Linda and I stepped inside, two men in bright smocks came toward us. The taller of the two extended his right hand. "I'm John," he said, shaking my hand first, then Linda's. "And that's Terry. We're here to help you get settled in." His smile kept me feeling at ease. Everyone and everything seemed so inviting and friendly. Not at all what I expected a mental institution to be.

Terry motioned to us from across the lobby. Linda and I headed that way while John brought up the rear, carrying my bag. As we reached Terry, he quickly turned a key on two windowless white doors that opened automatically in our direction. Stepping into the sterile hallway on the other side, I once again felt apprehension settle into my frazzled brain.

I stood waiting.

What have I done? I thought, trying not to let panic spread from my thoughts to my face. I didn't want Linda to worry. But relaxing seemed very out of the question in that moment.

The deadbolt dropped into place. I winced, though I hoped nobody saw me.

Linda tucked her arm under mine from behind. She saw me. What a relief. Her touch brought me back into the moment and gave me the assurance that everything would be okay. I took a deep breath, and we continued on down the hall with Terry and John.

The smells and sounds of the cafeteria hit me like a wall. Sensory overload! I wanted to hide. If I could have walked out the door beyond the lobby unnoticed, I would have. But I couldn't. I was on display. I felt every eye scan me from head to toe. I wondered which was worse, having everyone see you or being in a room full of people and having no one see you.

I felt Linda give my arm another everything-will-be-okay squeeze. "You can do this, Ray. I know you can." I stood and faced my new adventure with as much confidence as I could muster. A room full of alcoholics, drug abusers and mental patients. Welcome to Westbrook. The only place on earth where being different just makes you one of the crowd.

"Here, Ray, we ordered you a nice hot meal." Terry's voice broke through my thoughts as he handed me a supper tray. "Take your time. Linda can sit with you, if you'd like. When you're finished, we'll get you checked in." These guys really were so kind. In fact, every staff member we had come across so far had welcomed us with a smile, and not the fake kind. They seemed genuine and eager to serve us.

I determined to make the most of my visit here. It was an opportunity for a fresh start. Exactly what I needed.

As the crowd in the cafeteria began to filter out, I started feeling a little fidgety again. I knew Linda would be leaving soon. I wanted to be leaving too. But my strong, resilient wife stood firm. She knew this was best for me and for our family.

"I'll see you tomorrow," she said as she leaned in for a good-bye kiss. "I love you."

And away she went, straight toward the door, stopping only once for a quick wave. Before I knew it, Linda and her nurse escort disappeared through the tall, windowless doors and into the lobby. The familiar sound of the latch falling into place on the lock echoed down the hallway.

Surrounded by people, I felt for an instant the hollow pit of loneliness. My mind began to shoot all kinds of questions into the air. *What's next? Where should I go? What will be expected of me? Will I be able to do everything required of me? What if I can't?*

"Okay, Ray. Let's get you checked in." John picked up my bag and nodded the direction of the door.

My tenseness eased as the admission process began. This hospital was staffed by the nicest people. Everyone explained the routines carefully and made sure I signed all the right papers in all the right places. I sat through an extensive interview, answering question on top of question, explaining my surgeries, giving them contact information, describing some of my symptoms. I knew all the questions were in my best interest, but they wore me out! At one point my psychiatrist came in, nodded, grabbed my chart, and began writing orders without saying much.

Meanwhile, John went through my belongings, touching every stitch of every item I packed. I watched as he removed the nail clippers, comb, razor, and shaving cream from my satchel and put them into a bin labeled with my name. He checked each one of my pockets, practically turning them inside out, insuring I carried nothing sharp or harmful to myself or to another patient. Then came a private strip search.

Oddly, I felt relieved. Though everything was unfamiliar and in some ways humiliating, I knew I was in a safe place. I couldn't hurt myself or anyone else, especially my family. I was on the road to getting help.

With the process of admission completed, John could escort me to my room. I was exhausted, but I still had enough energy to be cordial enough to greet my roommate. He seemed a good bit younger than me and in great shape, perhaps from working out or playing sports as I used to be able to do.

"Hey ya, Ray, I'm Jack. Welcome to Westbrook," he said. "Good to meet you."

I stood in the middle of our room to take in the contents, making note of where John put my things. It seemed ordinary enough. Two single beds, each with its own nightstand and lamp, and two tall wardrobes. I unpacked, stuck my bag in the bottom of the wardrobe, and pretty quickly crawled into bed.

"Good night, Jack. See you in the morning."

Lying flat on my back, I pulled the blankets up to my neck, folded my arms across my chest and stared at the ceiling. For hours. Fighting back fearful thoughts and threatening voices.

This was going to be no vacation.

Very early the next morning, I saw one of the staff social workers. The intensity of my constant cycling required immediate attention. In fact, I saw this social worker twice that first day for thirty minutes each session. Plagued by instability, I experienced zero control of my emotions and little over my speech. The rapid shifting had never been this severe.

Making the adjustment to life behind locked doors didn't seem to be going well. I was fuzzy headed, I missed my Linda, and somebody always seemed to be staring at me. Everywhere I went, a nurse or attendant stood in the middle of the room with a clipboard, ready to record anything out of the ordinary.

The unfamiliarity of the environment would have been enough to keep me on edge. But constant prodding, the strict routine I couldn't grasp, and all the watchful eyes sent me within myself.

Hiding—my safe place, even in a crowd. Ever since I was a kid.

I yearned for something familiar, even from the start. If I could just get comfortable with one thing, maybe I could manage to deal better with every other thing.

I sought peace in the noise of the activity room. Hiding should be easy there. Suddenly a sweet familiar face showed up in the doorway. Linda! I'm telling you, I was never so happy to see her even though it had only been a day! But she didn't seem as happy to see me. My wife seemed almost scared of me. She just stood in one place until I got about ten feet away.

"What's in the bag? Something for me?" I reached out my hand. She took it. Then she relaxed and the sweetness returned to her face.

"I thought maybe you'd want to do some swimming."

"My trunks!" Oh, how I loved my sweet, sweet Linda. She always took care of me. What a wonderful reunion we had that day, and every day after that for the remainder of my time at Westbrook. I could never have managed one day in the dreaded battle of this illness without her standing by my side.

Over the first few days at the hospital, a therapist continued to observe me, making note of every behavior and conversation. He did some tests and spent time watching me in various group situations.

With the help of these notes and his own observations, my psychiatrist soon gave me a diagnosis: "I believe what we're looking at here, Ray, is atypical bipolar manic depression."

I stared for a good long while into the silence. Then I began to laugh. Uncontrollably. And tears came. Then the sobbing.

Somewhere in the daze of those minutes, I heard the doctor say, "There is no real cure. But we can do drug therapy to even out your mood swings."

I don't remember much he said after that. I took the pills someone handed me. I didn't want to. I wanted to crawl under the covers in bed and stay there for a good long while.

Eventually I began to respond to the medications, which included Navane and lithium carbonate. I recognized myself emerging from the cloudiness that had plagued me for months. Living within the limits of locked wards and observant staff became easier. I grew more and more aware of the other patients, taking note of their behaviors and wondering why some of them were so mean to the others. I guess because of my father, I was very sensitive when quiet people got bullied by others who made themselves boss.

I was helpful and responsive to the staff, often making them laugh with my side comments. I told one attendant, "I'm only in here to spy on you and give a report."

She raised one eyebrow and grinned. "Oh, you are? Well, I don't see anything wrong with you at all!"

I shrugged and wondered what would make anyone pretend to have atypical bipolar disease. It wouldn't be a very glamorous job.

Everything we did at Westbrook centered around getting us back to functioning well in society. To help with that, every one of us was given a specific responsibility within our community. I helped orient new patients coming into the ward. It was a good fit for me, since everyone thought I was the friendliest one in our group.

I liked to participate in athletic activities, so I got to meet a lot of people. I'll never forget the beautiful, billowing voice of an African-American preacher in treatment for alcoholism. He sang old hymns that echoed as we swam in the Olympic-sized swimming pool. Along with swimming, I worked out with weights every day and played basketball, volleyball, and even horseshoes in structured groups. The hospital offered other group therapy—music therapy and creative crafting—which I also participated in. But I preferred the athletic activities. They helped me stay in shape and gave me an outlet for the pent-up energy my body created.

Sixteen days of medication, observation, and intense therapy went by before the hospital released me. I felt better than I had in months, and I hoped beyond hope that the worst of my days were behind me.

I returned to work as a machinist and discovered that my favorite part of the work had become a thorn in my side—the precision. Micrometers that measured in tolerances of 0.001, one-thousandth of an inch, allowed no margin for error. While medication helped my brain be less fuzzy, it did not cure all my symptoms. I had to concentrate especially hard to remember measurements.

It became impossible to duplicate the metal parts I saw on the blueprints, to follow every step with accuracy as I had done before. The combination of the meds and being worn out from such intense concentration made me terribly sleepy. I couldn't bring a job all the way to completion. My co-workers saw my difficulties, felt bad, and tried to cover for me. But one afternoon they caught me dozing and asked me to please see the plant doctor, and I did.

Between him and my psychiatrist, they began sending me on bouts of sick leave. I became extremely frustrated, and they knew it. But they really had no choice.

After I suffered through this yo-yo pattern throughout the summer, my psychiatrist sat down with me during one of my sessions to go over some difficult news. "You're not going to like what I have to tell you," he said. "I want you to retire."

I began to stage a loud protest.

But the doctor interrupted me. "If you don't retire, Ray, you'll lose everything. Your job. Your benefits. Your dignity. I've seen it happen to too many people."

"But I love what I do. I've done it with excellence for nearly twenty years."

"You and Linda need to talk this over and give it some serious thought. I hope you'll take my recommendation."

Dealing with shame, remorse, and the fear of being ostracized due to the social stigma of mental illness, we took as much time as we could to make our decision. We had the boys to think about too. College to help with. Scott was a senior and Adam was in the ninth grade. And what about our medical bills and other expenses? It all seemed too overwhelming. The enemy's lies were hard at work, making us think we had to have everything figured out.

In the fall of 1992, Linda and I reluctantly went to the Social Security office so I could apply for disability benefits. We were both devastated. Sadness filled the quiet between us. We mourned the loss of the life we once had together. The joy. The laughter. How could this be happening? We were supposed to be young and vibrant! Filled with love and delight in serving the Lord.

Not now. Maybe not ever.

As the new year rolled by, I used up my vacation time as well as my sick leave. And on February 10, 1993, I officially retired from Aqualon after nearly twenty years of service. Me. Ray Sturt. A retiree. What do you think about that?

With the wind of work out of my sails, I bought into the idea of becoming a couch potato. My lounge chair became my comfort. With my defenses down and the enemy on the move, I settled into severe depression and growing discouragement. Fifteen pounds later and flailing once again from the bottom of a pit, I also had to find a new psychiatrist. Evidently, psychiatrists experience crisis too, and sometimes they even run from it. Mine had divorced his wife, remarried, closed his practice, and moved away.

So back to the work of finding a suitable doctor to walk me through this jungle. My mind flashed back to boot camp and the soldiers who fought in the thick vegetation of Vietnam. I wished I still had the ability to maneuver around these obstacles on my own. But I didn't. Not anymore. I needed help. The enemy had squeezed me tight, up into another corner. I had no strength left to stand. All I could do is lean. And wait.

The first doctor we went to decided he needed Linda to validate everything I said. Now, I didn't understand this method of therapy, but there I sat, under his faulty influence and stuck with paying him my dollar. For weeks Linda and I met together with this man, trying to give him the benefit of the doubt. He never did earn it. He didn't believe a single thing I said. Before long, this psychiatrist up and moved his practice all the way to Texas. Why he'd leave the beauty of the mid South, I will never know. But away he went.

Grasping at straws, I began to look for a new psychiatrist. Again. I called my old roommate from Westbrook and asked him about his doctor. Jack went on and on about his credentials, including fourteen years of higher education and his noteworthy reputation among his peers in psychiatric research.

From the minute Linda and I walked into this doctor's office, we were impressed by his level of expertise. The walls held so many diplomas and distinguished-service awards, they looked like wallpaper hanging around the room. Well-groomed and distinguished-looking, the doctor met us at the door and made us feel very welcome. His caring demeanor gave him an unusual ability to listen sympathetically and to offer wisdom.

He saw me in a way few other doctors have. Not just what I told him, but the things in the background that I didn't say. There was no awkward silence. I felt no need to hide. In fact, the doctor seemed to be impressed with my insight and perspective on this illness. When I asked about altering the dosages of my medications, he heard me. And he agreed. He valued my input and made me feel as though I had at least some say.

Bipolar disorder dictated most aspects of my life. It required multiple medications, most with significant side effects. Monitoring the dosages closely helped to keep some of the side effects under control. Over the years I got good at juggling. At one point or another, I tried Moban, Klonopin, Ritalin, Risperdal, Zyprexa, Celexa, thioridazine, Geodon, and Trileptal. Lithium carbonate and Depakote served as anchors, especially during the acute times of my illness.

Still, pressure mounted. I continued to cycle through highs and lows. Some episodes brought on surges of power, as if there were electrodes attached to my brain. Most episodes landed me in an extreme depression.

Despite three thousand milligrams of medicine per day, my brain held on to its bipolar symptoms with a tight fist. I could do nothing to loosen its grip. Every breath became a labored attempt at life. A life I was losing.

Finally, I concocted one last-ditch experiment during an especially insufferable season. I heard somewhere that taking a shot of straight scotch might help. Drinking had never been my style, but I was desperate and looking for any kind of relief I could find. So I did exactly what had been suggested. With Adam and his friend Hank watching, I poured three ounces of scotch, tipped my head back, and sucked down the contents of the glass in one big gulp. The liquid stung all the way to the gullet.

The scotch didn't even take the edge off my symptoms. But I could see how the numbing effect of several drinks might take the edge off how much I cared. No wonder so many suffering from bipolar disorder become alcoholics and drug addicts. They will do whatever drastic measure it takes to bring even the smallest amount of relief.

The mental anguish of bipolar disorder can strike anyone, from professional football players to talented musicians or blue-collar folks like me. Some—like the genius Ernest Hemingway, who shot himself, or Virginia Woolf, who filled her pockets with rocks and sank to the bottom of a river—give up their lives to this monster of an illness.

Others, like Carrie Fisher who played Princess Leia in *Star Wars,* fight the extreme of an unseen enemy due to being undiagnosed. In an interview by Diane Sawyer on *Primetime* several years ago[2], she said, "I used to think I was a drug addict, pure and simple, just someone who could not stop taking drugs willfully. And I was that. But it turns out that I am severely manic depressive." It took Carrie twenty years and a mental breakdown to say this out loud in front of the public. She described periods of frenzied thoughts with night after night of not sleeping.

I'm telling you, I knew what she meant. Her honesty gave me insight and understanding that I couldn't see when I was in the middle of the hard seasons. She told of trying to hide her darkest places from her Hollywood friends with endless monologues and constant chatter. "I have two moods," she explained. "One is rollicking Roy, the wild ride of a mood. And sediment Pam stands on the shore and sobs. Sometimes the tide is in; sometimes it's out. I would call my friends and say, 'Roy's in town!' They all loved Roy. But the other mood, Pam, doesn't answer the phone."

Because of her brilliance, everybody bought into this woman's illusion that everything was fine. She "believed" them herself until everything broke. She began hallucinating and landed in a psychiatric hospital, signing her admittance form "Shame" with her left hand.

After several months, Carrie left the hospital determined to keep the disease at bay. Often easier said than done! Admitting that relapse could occur at any time, she credits her six medications, time, acceptance of her condition, and the incredible support of doctors, family, and friends for her comeback. "I outlasted my problems …" she said. "I'm still surviving."

"Shame." I knew that place very well. It hung around my neck like one of those sandwich signs with barbells attached at the bottom. It may as well have been a millstone. So many of my responses toward my family were filtered first through this persona. Four-letter words spit from my mouth like arrows, striking Linda or the boys with their venom-dipped tips.

Episodes of anger, even rage, filled our days with misery. If I could have ended it all, I would have. Not just my own life, but the whole earth. "If I were God, I would do away with everything!" Me. Ray Sturt. God? How blasphemous can a man become? Feeling remorse, I got my Bible out to read, hoping to catch a glimmer of light. I got so agitated, I threw the Bible to the floor and staged a tantrum right on top of it. I know it hurt Linda. I watched her eyes well up. I felt this strange sensation of pride and grief, in conflict yet attempting to dance on the same floor.

"I don't know why God doesn't strike you down, Ray. If this hurts me, I know it hurts Him."

When Linda caught my eye just right, the grief would well up from deep inside me. But I didn't have the ability to respond from that place. It hovered there, waiting to be acknowledged. Instead, I would quote Romans 3:23 and blurt out in defense, "If He strikes me down, He'll have to strike down everyone. 'For all have sinned and fall short of the glory of God'!"

So high and mighty. But oh, how hard the prideful fall.

"How do you like it?" the salesman asked as I downshifted coming out of the curve. The smile on my face must have given away my response. He went right into his pitch. "Just put your check down, and I'll hold the car for you. Send me the rest of the money within the week, and the car will be yours."

Oh, yeah. Scott was going to love this car. A sporty little Nissan coupe. *Zoom!* Perfect for the college man. He would be so surprised when he got out of class and I told him about his sweet new ride. And Linda would beam with pride when she heard about my accomplishment.

Fueled first by the salesman and then by Scott's response when I met him after class, I could barely keep my foot off the accelerator on the drive home. I was so excited, I ran into the house and immediately began to spill all the details to my beloved wife.

"You did WHAT?" Linda didn't respond to my good news the way I thought she would.

My elation turned quickly to irritation as on and on she went. "Scott doesn't even know how to drive a stick shift! What would possess you to do such a thing? And you gave them a check, Ray? A check? For five hundred dollars? Well, you're just going to have to get it back. We are NOT buying Scott a sports car with a stick shift."

I can't remember Linda ever being so angry with me. But I knew exactly what possessed me. I was in a manic season, a season when I felt as light as air. Buying Scott that cool car made me feel unstoppable. It felt almost as good as driving the car itself, zipping around the curves. It made me feel as though I were in control. But spending money like this really indicated how out of control the manic in me could become.

The enemy of bipolar disorder masked itself in a lot of different ways. Entrapping me by making me feel good seemed terribly unfair and cruel. It used trickery to make me feel "normal," luring my brain into imagining all was right with my world.

All wasn't right with my world. I swallowed my pride, submitted to the extreme limitations of the bipolar siege with the help of my brave wife, and wrote a letter to the car dealership. I explained my condition, canceled the sale, and requested the check be returned.

Typically, after an extreme high like the experience of buying the sports car, I fell hard. The reality of depression would return with added doses of paranoia and confusion. They toppled me in the simplest of tasks. Like finding our car in the parking lot.

One afternoon Linda and I took off to go shopping at the mall, the same mall where we'd been shopping for years. On this particular day, we went to the lot after making our purchases, and I couldn't find our car. Literally. I found myself following closely behind my wife, parroting her.

When she stopped, I stopped. But not trusting her decision, I nervously looked up and down the rows of cars. Frustration turned to paranoia. Linda gave me a quick stare. In my highly volatile state, I proclaimed, "Linda, this is not our car!"

"Ray, this is our car."

My wife can be pretty persuasive. But that day nothing could persuade me. I walked around to the front of the car, studied the license plate, and walked back to where Linda stood waiting with her arms crossed.

I stared at her for a long while. Then suddenly, my dazed mind cleared like scales had fallen from my eyes. I tried not to show my embarrassment. I simply unlocked the doors so we could get in.

I sat, stunned, huddled behind the steering wheel, pretending no one else could see me. I waited a few seconds, took a deep breath, and started the car. We drove home in silence. But my mind was stirred up. I was scared.

Scared about what happened. Scared about what might have happened. Scared to be with people. Scared to be without people. Scared that some day I would be alone, backed into a corner by a merciless enemy, with no way out and no way to defend myself.

CHAPTER 8

ENGULFED

*Suffering is permanent, obscure and dark,
and shares the nature of infinity.*
—William Wordsworth

From Linda

As hours turned into days, I began to see that Ray was right where he needed to be. With the medications and attention in therapy, hints of his old demeanor began to emerge. He greeted me with smiles and hugs instead of blank stares or grunts.

The distance that had formed between Ray and me began to fall away. We started communicating again. Trusting. Believing. A lot of it had to do with the assurance that we were not the only family suffering under the siege of mental illness. Many people, from various walks of life, all dealing with debilitating issues, filled the hospital.

Through our separation and experiences at Westbrook, we recognized that we needed each other. This battle affected both of us. All of us. And neither of us was alone in the fight.

One of the fronts Ray faced almost immediately after coming home from the hospital turned out to be his job. In spite of his vacillating moods and threats before he left, he found that the guys at the shop received him back with open arms. (He's always been a good worker, personable and kind.) But the work in which he had taken so much pride in the past brought him back to the same heartache he felt just before going into the hospital. Lethargic from the medicine and often confused, he couldn't keep up or follow plans. Once he became aware that things weren't going well, his moods escalated, which made things worse. It got so bad that his friends could no longer cover for his mistakes.

He was devastated. Ray loved his job. He didn't just *build* machine parts, he *crafted* them to perfection. It was a heart thing for him, a source of identity and even ministry. He liked being able to contribute to the success of the company and to the lives of the people around him.

A great quote from St. Francis of Assisi describes Ray and the work he enjoyed. "He who works with his hands is a laborer. He who works with his hands and his head is a craftsman. He who works with his hands and his head and his heart is an artist." Ray wouldn't see himself this way, but I do. My Ray is an artist. Everything he does connects from his heart.

The day Ray filed for Social Security disability benefits, I knew the reality that my strong, compassionate Ray might not ever be able to hold a job again. Permanent disability at forty-three. Incomprehensible. The thought filled me with dread and fear. How was our family going to survive? My job was only part-time. Scott would need to enroll in college soon, with his brother not far behind. This was no time for the head of our household to retire!

But the choice wasn't mine or even Ray's. We had to learn to cope. Adjust to the unexpected turns in our lives. The years to follow would not be easy. After his retirement, Ray dealt with some dark, dark days. We all dealt with some dark, dark days. The hope I held in my hand when we left the hospital quickly scattered.

With his temper off the scale, Ray struck out with profanity and disgust, never physically touching any of us but bombarding us with verbal abuse. Those nasty words stuck in my brain. If I could have scrubbed it with a wire brush, I would have. My sweet, caring Ray tore me down, over and over and over. After twenty years, how could he talk to me like this?

This man meant the world to me. We had enjoyed our life together—gardening, playing tennis, enjoying television shows, raising our two boys, and teasing our dogs over the years. Life had been good.

Now, it was everything I could do some days to stay.

Ray's threats grew more cruel. His harsh tone cut like a knife straight through to my heart. I had no defense. Typically, I just stood there and took it, absorbing every pain-filled blow. I kept reminding myself that he was sick and would never talk to me like that if he were well.

When he started threatening to kill one of the boys or to kill me, however, I became especially frightened. I knew how volatile he could be. I needed to take those threats seriously. My sweet Ray was tormented, sun up to sun down. And I could do nothing to save him.

When he shared his thoughts of suicide or homicide, I trembled. What would happen to me? Would I live? Or would I die? I did my best to trust in God's protective care, and I reasoned that nothing would happen to me unless it was in God's sovereign will. I continued to pray for safety and contemplated leaving.

Ray and the boys used to enjoy watching *The Three Stooges*. Laughing together was one of our favorite things to do as a family. It helped us to remember to breathe. In one episode, the three men took on jobs with the government to help take the census. The comedy of their interactions with each other and with the people who answered the door made me laugh out loud. But it's one of Moe's questions that I remember. "Good morning, sir. I'm the census taker. Are you married or happy?" A woman's voice filtered in from the background, seeming to be nagging at the man who answered the door.

"Married," he grunted, as he shrugged and motioned his head toward the source of the voice. I laughed at the humor, but it also made me a little sad. I loved being married. My marriage to Ray had always been a source of happiness. The two weren't separate in my mind.

I couldn't imagine not being married to Ray. So every time he asked me for a divorce, I cringed. My heart broke, though I always said no.

"But I don't know what love is anymore," he would reply.

"No, Ray."

"But I don't think I can love anymore. Love is only a feeling," he insisted.

"No, Ray. I am as committed to you today as I was the day I married you."

My response to Ray, when pressed, was always to support him. But sometimes I wasn't sure I meant it. I wrestled with God a lot about this. I felt like a kept woman. A time came when I knew in my heart that I needed to make a decision once and for all. I prayed and I prayed. Day and night I prayed, *Lord, You know my needs and the needs of my family. I give them to You. You alone can fill the emptiness and give me what I need to stay in my marriage, no matter what. If it's going to be for life, it's going to have to be You. You have to do it.*

I listened to God's heart and read His Word. I found this instruction: "Above all, love each other deeply, because love covers over a multitude of sins" (1 Pet. 4:8). I wrote it on a card and placed it over my sink. And I clung to those words.

I would not be leaving my husband. I knew God's heart toward Ray, and toward me, was unconditional love. *Above all, love each other deeply. Above all, love each other deeply.* I would take a deep breath every time I said it and remember to submit myself to the Lord, and to Ray, in love. Even through the infliction of pain, the abuse, the threats, I would love Ray, with God's help, no matter what.

I made the decision to stay, which filtered my responses toward Ray, but it didn't make things easy. I went through a period of mourning, as if the husband I married had died. The grief would wash over me, and I'd find myself huddled in a corner, covered in extreme sadness. Where was my Ray? I wanted him back. But I knew he would never be back.

With God's help, I accepted Ray's erratic behavior and his unpredictable moods as a part of him. And I began to once again love him. This new man. My Ray.

This time, when Ray tried to push me toward divorce, I stood my ground, and I meant it. "I love you, Ray. I will not ever divorce you. No matter how many times you ask. Even if you bring me divorce papers, I won't sign them. And you can't make me."

Through this whole ordeal with Ray, God never failed to show His faithfulness. He became someone I could rely on moment by moment. I discovered that I could cling to Him, and cling I did. To Him alone. God invited me to be His bride, and I accepted. He was my number one, even over my husband.

Living with Ray and accepting him for who he was now required some adjustments on my part. On rare days, most often when we were on vacation, I hardly noticed Ray was sick. He opened doors, spoke in nice tones, and ate with me at the dinner table. But on other days, he wore "irritable" all over his face and up and down both sleeves. On those days, with behavior typical for someone suffering from manic-depressive disorder, he turned on me like a snake. I learned not to argue with him and not to give my opinion unless it was absolutely necessary. Frequently, I retreated to the bedroom to watch television or read while he was in the family room downstairs.

One of the most difficult things for me proved to be allowing Ray space. I loved my strong, kind man. I liked being up close to him. We were comfortable in each other's space from the night of our first date. Transparent and real and close. It challenged me terribly not to put my hand in his when we walked somewhere together and not to sit up against him on the couch while we watched television. Even on his good nights, Ray didn't engage much. It made him extra jittery if he didn't have space to move freely.

Ray often yelled at me over our food. I cooked nourishing meals, but they were never quite right. Too dark, too light. Too brown, too red. Too sweet, not sweet enough. Or he wouldn't want to eat at all after I'd cooked. Between his medications and the depression, his appetite dropped. He was less active than he ever used to be, and he went through periods of falling asleep a lot when he sat down to watch television.

I confess that I did not always have a patient spirit. Ray's hurtful comments would sometimes get under my skin and send me over the edge. I snapped at him many times. One time I even shouted across the room at him as he walked away, "You're just an a—hole and you'll die an a—hole!" I wasn't very proud of that one.

Sometimes the silent treatment was the only tactic I had against his constant commenting and verbal pushing. The silence got under his skin. He struggled with it. I struggled without it.

I fought not only the battle of Satan's attacks on me through Ray, but I also dealt with battles against my own flesh. Weariness grew in me, and I struggled to stay on top of everything falling to me. Some things fell to me by choice, others by default.

With Ray's mind and body denying him the ability to manage much in the operation of our household, a great deal of it fell to me—the checkbook, taxes, budgeting and other finances, and legal and medical issues, all on top of everyday responsibilities. After my mom's heart surgery, she needed around-the-clock care. I hired someone to stay in her home, but I took care of her laundry and did all of her grocery shopping.

Then in the fall of 1995, I received a call of distress from the dean at Shenandoah University, where Scott was in his third semester. He insisted that we pick him up right away and get him in for a psychiatric evaluation. Scott had begun pacing frequently, grimacing, and having issues with flight of thought.

Ray and I picked him up, along with all of his belongings and his Thunderbird. Two weeks later he received a diagnosis: bipolar disorder.

My son, creative and smart and full of life, burdened with a mental illness at the young age of twenty-one. The news nearly knocked my feet out from under me. After all I had been through with Ray, I didn't know whether I would be able to walk with my son in the way I hoped I could. I spent energy way faster than I could refuel.

But I added Scott to the top of my priorities and began juggling his doctor appointments right along with my mom's and Ray's. I continued working at the hospital two or three days a week, doing everything I could for everybody I loved with little left over for myself. I could feel my stress levels nearing the saturation mark.

"How do you do it, Mrs. Sturt?" one of Scott's doctors asked me.

"I pray. All day, every day. I live one day at a time, sometimes one hour at a time. And I try to laugh a lot."

The doctor smiled and nodded, almost as if to say, "Sure you do." Then he offered a good piece of advice: "Mrs. Sturt, you need to make time for yourself in any way you can and take a break from your circumstances." He suggested that I try to get away. I smiled and nodded.

As the demands on me mounted, the enemy's pressure increased. I began to experience fatigue like I'd never known. Not just a need-a-nap kind of tired, but a deep-seated weariness that left me depleted of any strength whatsoever. And I began to ache all over. The pain settled in and didn't leave. It kept me from sleeping well and distracted me throughout the day. Finally, my doctor referred me to a rheumatologist. He diagnosed me with fibromyalgia.

"The good news? It won't kill you. But the bad news is that it will make you feel like you want to die." He prescribed a regimen of heat and exercise along with pills to help me sleep deeply. I took them.

Ray became increasingly fragmented, and I sank ever deeper into the background. I was in danger of being engulfed by the weariness of the work of being Ray's wife, Scott and Adam's mom, my mother's daughter, the patients' nurse, and caregiver for our new golden retriever puppy, Sophie.

A recent commercial for the drug Seroquel reveals the sadness of men and women blending into the background of the environments surrounding them. It opens with a woman sitting on a sofa, despondent, as her children play around her. From the neck down the pattern of her clothing blends with the squared effect of the sofa's fabric. "When you're living with bipolar depression, it's easy to feel like you're fading into the background. That's because bipolar depression doesn't just affect you, it can consume you …"

While the image represents someone who suffers from the disease, I see myself on that couch. Bipolar illness consumes not just an individual patient but his entire family. And no amount of medication will cure the intense sadness and feelings of hiddenness.

I longed to be seen as Linda. To be known. To be among the living. I had been among the walking dead far too long.

My honest, intimate conversations with God began, *Revive me.* Burdened with the loneliness of being years in church without Ray, I cried inwardly and prayed, *Revive me.* Through torrents of tears, begging for my family's deliverance, I cried out, *Father, revive me! Use me for Your glory. I long to see You work. In me. In my husband. In my boys. Use us for Your glory.*

In February 2002, with Ray's surprising permission, half a dozen women began coming into our home to study the Bible and pray. My soul had experienced a long, dry season. The conversations with these women around our dining-room table refreshed and inspired me. They inspired all of us. We read through Ephesians over the first several weeks, discussing it verse by verse, taking as little or as long as we needed in each section. We became prayer partners. And these women became like a shield, protecting and strengthening me through an intense summer season.

Ray experienced several bad episodes, some while we were in Virginia Beach at the condo. From time to time during manic episodes, Ray's mind raced, reaching extreme highs and stealing away sleep. He probably could have conquered the world. Instead, he left the condo, intent on conquering eight flights of stairs to talk with the night-shift guard. Each entertained the other to pass the night away.

Ray's energy often came like a gust of wind, blowing in unexpectedly. Thankfully, he enjoyed walking and riding his bike along the oceanside trail. He just had to ride out his periods of mania. And so did we.

Scott and Adam were deeply concerned about their dad's behavior. More accurately, they were worried about me. I expressed to them my acceptance of their dad's disorder as a part of the whole man, to love and cherish and walk through life with. They understood and even agreed. Together we decided the next day's activities and asked Ray to join us, and he did.

We had great fun at the water park, challenging each other on the miniature golf course, buzzing around the track in motorcars at the miniature raceway, and flying down the waterslides on rubber mats. We were all dragging at the end of the day.

In the evenings we walked along the water's edge down to Rudee inlet, dodging the waves along the way. Giggles followed every splash or accidental soaking. Seagulls danced through the air, diving to snatch up bits of bread and other morsels left behind by sunbathers earlier in the day. Small yachts and fishing boats made their way back to dock for the night through the inlet. Each one slowed suddenly when the NO WAKE signs came into view. We laughed at the spectacle of the parade, especially the boys. They loved the times we shared as a family.

Ray had invested a lot of time with Scott and Adam, especially when they were younger. I wished he could see them for the young men they had become, in large part because of him. He may have caught glimpses on good days and appreciated them in short spurts of awareness. But I never knew whether he could comprehend something abstract like that and connect all the dots.

They wanted to give back to him, love on him in their own way. But he was often like a porcupine and unable to let anyone near him. It affected them. It affected all of us. But we agreed that we loved Ray more than we hated the disorder that seemed to hold us all captive in some way.

When we returned to the condo after a full day of fun, Scott and Adam settled down with a movie and some popcorn. Some nights they challenged their dad and me to a game of Uno, Yahtzee, or Aggravation. We laughed together into the late night hours and went to bed content and grateful.

I grew more and more accustomed to seeing Ray as a whole person in spite of the expectations of people around us. At the end of the summer, a close childhood friend of mine said to me, "You know that God can heal Ray." My jaw dropped.

"Yes, I know that God can heal Ray," I rattled off in quick response. "But He's not going to heal him. Ray has manic depression, and it's in his genes." I wished that people would see Ray as I saw him, including his illness. Bipolar disorder may have changed him, but it didn't define him.

Fall came, and the wind grew cold. So too did Ray. A dark depression settled in and clung to his bones. Talk of suicide once again filled his thoughts and his conversations. I feared for him.

All I could do was lean into the Lord as my Protector, my Deliverer. Our Deliverer.

Lord, Ray belongs to You. You bought him with a price. Hold on to him even when I can't.

CHAPTER 9

SURRENDER EXPLORED

*How long must I wrestle with my thoughts
and every day have sorrow in my heart?*
—Psalm 13:2

The enemy pressed in on me, threatening my lifeline, shutting down relationships, intensifying the chaos in my mind. He backed me right into a corner. It's true, what they say about being backed into a corner. You'll choose either fight or flight. The conflict between the two left me with neither. Though I was ready to give in, let go, and give my family some peace.

Even Sophie suffered from my extremes. The medication affected my balance at times, and she easily got under foot. I tripped over her sprawling, lanky legs one too many times. My patience was thin. Very thin. One afternoon, on my way upstairs with arms full of groceries, I lost my balance and stumbled over her outstretched limbs. She was sleeping so peacefully on the cool floor of the hallway. Nearly falling, I blew out, "Why in the #@!#@! don't you move, dog! You're always in my way!" Then I kicked her. If not for Linda rescuing her, I could have hurt her without much effort.

I had been mild mannered for most of my life, but now manic episodes became more frequent, cursing me with near-brute strength and electrified energy. I barely recognized myself. It's no wonder the neighbors went running for shelter when they saw me coming. I felt like a hideous monster, not unlike the Incredible Hulk from the television series that aired in the seventies.

While I didn't feel the change coming on like David Banner did, the effects of the manic stage often left a path of destruction. One afternoon a lovely couple from church stopped by the house to reach out to us in kindness. They came to the door, and I lost it, ripping them with ugly language and general rudeness. Intruders. Scum of the earth. Worse. I'll never forget the look of horror on their faces. Thinking back on it makes me feel sad. I wasn't a mean, hurtful person. But that's who they saw. Full force. I wondered whether my repulsion of people had to do with trying to keep from them the ugliness that had become my constant companion.

Friends stopped coming by. Neighbors stopped being neighborly. One lady added an extra dead bolt to her side door that faced our house after she observed my outbursts. She was especially terrified at night. If I happened to be in my back yard and her dogs were out in her fenced yard, she called them into the garage. I couldn't contain the turmoil to my mind when manic hit me.

In my short spurts of sanity, I would see the horror and feel the judgement and experience the isolation. It made me call out from somewhere deep, "I am not an animal!" though my cry went unheard.

I felt twisted and contorted. Everyone saw me. No one understood me. I wanted to hide in the safety of silence as I did when I was a kid. But I couldn't. Isolation became my preferred manner of life. But it didn't keep people from noticing me.

One night, while I was out jogging along our road—I even took my workout time under the cloak of darkness—a guy pulled up behind me with his friend in the car and flipped on his bright lights. They wanted a good look at the crazed man who only came out of his house at night, I guess. He yelled questions out his window as if I were deaf. "Hey freak! How about showing us how strong you are, huh?"

On nights like that, I imagined myself as the Hulk, saying, "You won't like me when I'm angry" before grabbing on to the bumper of the car and hoisting it over my head just for kicks. Then I'd toss the car with the nosy teenagers into a nearby field. Somehow the thought brought momentary satisfaction. But also a deep sadness.

God had not given me a dark spirit, but a thoughtful one. This illness had taken over everything of worth and value in my life. I wanted to slay the demons inside me. I threatened many times. The more I threatened, the more they tormented.

Late one night, while Linda was still out working at the hospital, I decided to try and still my mind by sitting alone in the quiet of our upstairs bedroom. I turned the television off and kicked up the footrest of my recliner. But my mind found anything but rest. Every time I started to close my eyes, something in the hallway drew my attention. I couldn't imagine what it could be, as I was alone. An uneasiness moved into my spirit. I stared at the doorway, trying to discern what I was seeing pass back and forth. As my eyes focused, I recognized the outline of a human-shaped form. Ghostly. Floating. This couldn't be happening. I tried desperately to wake up from what I thought was a nightmare.

I wasn't asleep.

"Ray ... Ray." A female voice called to me. I went to the door, hoping to find that Linda had come home. She hadn't. More voices joined in the calling. The apparitions came at me, pushing me back. I could no longer make out what they were saying. Chaos filled the room. I pulled a blanket from my bed and wrapped myself in it. Gasping for breath, I slunk to the floor, violently shaking my head, trying to keep the voices at bay. *This can't be happening.*

"Go away. ... Please, just leave me alone." Fear filled me in a way I had never before experienced. I could feel the life draining from my body, from my spirit. Apparitions surrounded me, their whispers incessant, their breaths slow and torturous. *Could this be death?*

Morning came. I buried my disappointment and drew in a breath, involuntarily admitting to life.

Life, at the time, meant little to me. I may have been breathing, but I sure wasn't living. The apparitions haunted me, taking away the thread of peace I had left. I never knew when they might appear. I could trust nothing to be real when such a percentage of what I perceived existed only to me. The doorbell would ring but no one would be waiting at the door to come in. I disliked being alone, and I no longer connected consistently with Linda.

I begged her to let me go. Begged her. At times, I threatened her. Yes, I threatened my wife. The woman who brought such delight into my sad-storied life. I experienced nothing but sadness or anger around her. Sometimes even rage. I envied her calmness and ability to manage without much help from me.

I had it in me to unleash a whole lot of damage. On good days, which were fewer and farther between, the potential terrified me. I didn't want to discover the lengths to which I'd be willing to go to exterminate the torment in my mind.

Relief from the fury came in short blasts of pleasure. In the early days of summer, cool morning breezes set the stage for warm afternoons. Linda and I enjoyed opening up all the windows and sitting in the quiet of our family room. The sensation of the air on my skin seemed to bring short segments of peace and allowed a few minutes of civil conversation between the two of us.

In the middle of just such a morning, flames started shooting across the patio door! I panicked and jumped up to get the water pitcher from the refrigerator. "Linda, find the phone and call the fire department!"

"Why do I need to call the fire department?"

I stopped mid rush and looked at Linda's face. Calm. Not an ounce of concern showed in her expression. "Look! There's a fire on the patio!"

SURRENDER EXPLORED

Her expression changed. I've seen it before. It was a picture of her broken heart. She didn't see the flames. There were none.

I ran to the doorway with the water, flames still dancing in my mind.

"Ray, there is no fire."

"How can you be sure unless you come out here and look?"

"But there is no fire, Ray. Please, come sit down."

No fire? But the flames ... they were so real. I stepped out to the patio. Linda was right. There was no fire. I went back into the house and slunk into my overstuffed armchair, glancing over to the doorway, expecting another blaze to flare up.

The enemy taunted me. I could hear him laughing, see him pointing. *Oh, God. How long must I wrestle with my thoughts and every day have sorrow in my heart?* (Ps. 13:2). I hadn't turned to God in over a decade. Not once. I wondered whether He would even still know me.

I was at the bottom of the barrel. What did I have to lose? I tried calling on God's name to help me on days I was coherent. Sometimes I called out to Him when unusual phenomenon like the flames reminded me that my battle wasn't just against my flesh or my brain, but against the devil. I don't recall expecting any results. I simply had nowhere else to turn.

Darkness continued to hover over me like storm clouds settling in over a mountaintop. Crisp details ran together like dripping paint mixed with too much water. Hints of light emerged when the clouds shifted, but all too quickly they shifted again, leaving me in complete darkness. The glimpses gave me hope, but not for healing. For the possibility of a life lived in the gaps.

I wondered whether I might be able to surrender. Fear consumed me, but I didn't see any other choice. If I could surrender to the life I'd been given, perhaps I could salvage a few more moments with my wife or some new conversations with my sons. I missed my sons. I wanted Linda back in my arms. Was I willing to fight for the family I loved? Would I wind up hurting them even more deeply than I already had? I wasn't sure I could take the risk.

A drowning man can't worry about the risk of the fight when he's consumed with where in the world he's going to find his next breath. I needed a life preserver, and I knew it. How could I signal for help when my lungs were already filling with water? It was too late. I was going down. Me. Ray Sturt. Strong, athletic, a swimmer, once a God follower, a good husband and dad, drowning. Too tired to fight.

In spite of faithfully meeting with my psychiatrist, regularly taking my medication, and being steeped in the prayers of an amazing family, I struggled to maintain some sense of reality during the bulk of every single day. Despair grew. I felt utterly frustrated and profoundly faithless.

Years earlier, as a young follower of Christ, I memorized a Scripture verse that I thought would carry me through any dilemma that came my way. "And we know that in all things God works for the good of those who love him, who have been called according to his purpose" (Rom. 8:28). Recalling it now made my stomach churn. *Called.* For what? Spewing evil all over the people I loved? Even if I was a child of God, I didn't see any good coming from the extreme shades of darkness my mental illness represented.

I felt lost and utterly alone. But according to one of my favorite authors, George Muller, a man of devout faith and deep prayer who founded orphanages in Bristol on nothing but spare change, I shouldn't have. "Be assured," he wrote, "if you walk with Him [God], and look to Him, and expect help from Him, He will never fail you."[3] I had walked faithfully with God, looked to Him for help, loved my family, and persevered in my illness the best I could. But in the end, all I could think was that He failed me.

SURRENDER EXPLORED

I tried to believe in God's sovereignty, but year after year the siege of this bipolar disorder took its toll. My family suffered so much. If not for Linda, we would have been ripped apart. I didn't understand why God chose to be silent. I could not recall a time in the years the disorder had owned my life when my condition brought glory to God. I'm uncertain whether I deemed Him undeserving or myself unworthy. Likely, it was a combination of the two.

CHAPTER 10

UNEXPECTED LIFELINE

God doesn't just throw a life preserver to a drowning person. He goes to the bottom of the sea, and pulls a corpse from the bottom of the sea, takes him up on the bank, breathes into him the breath of life and makes him alive.
—R. C. Sproul

The fury of the earth continued to unleash itself in front of my eyes, stretching my faith and challenging my belief in the sovereignty of God. Thoughts of suicide pushed their way to the front of my mind more and more frequently. The manic episodes began to taper off, but the severity and length of my depressed seasons grew. I fought hard to keep open the windows of opportunity for living in the gap. I desperately wanted to engage in the lives of my family, but it was becoming difficult.

Scott struggled with the onset of bipolar disorder. Linda worried, uncertain of how I would respond to her. Adam wanted to move into his grown-up life as a musician but couldn't quite seem to make a go of it in our hometown. I could do very little to support the people I loved on a daily basis. So when windows showed a crack, I surrendered myself to the moments at hand, knowing they would be fleeting.

In the fall of 2001, an opportunity opened up for Adam that required an out-of-state move. Linda and I were thrilled, and I was given a sliver of sanity, so I snagged it. On September 8, we loaded up my old '81 Ford pickup and Adam's '99 Mazda with all of his earthly possessions. Then we hit the road south, headed toward an old farmhouse in Wake Forest, North Carolina. Adam's close friend and mentor had recently completed seminary and received a masters degree from Duke University. He was off to Oxford to study for his doctorate on a full scholarship, leaving his job and his home available. He had offered both to Adam. Once we got him set up in the house, Adam would be teaching private guitar lessons at a music store in Raleigh, just a short drive from his new home.

When we walked into the tall white structure sitting among the cornfields of North Carolina, tears filled my eyes. Imperfect and in need of some repairs, this house, built around 1900, would be my son's first home. What a wonderful gift this was for him … for all of us. Of course, I had a hard time expressing my feelings to Adam in that moment. I think the tears came from a grateful heart. The last ten years or so had not been easy. My illness had stolen time and brought heartache. But that day I saw the generous heart of God toward my son. The gesture spoke to me of hope. This was a sweet example of surrendering to the life I'd been given, ready to receive the gift of life that came in the gaps.

I wondered briefly whether suffering might be a gift in and of itself, leading me to an extraordinary awareness of what matters in life.

UNEXPECTED LIFELINE

Grateful for the uninterrupted time with Adam, we set about unpacking and getting his new home in order. The soaring ceilings and uninsulated walls would require some creative means of keeping the house warm in the winter. I did everything I could to help with the efficiency of the heating system. We made sure the fireplace was sealed off to the damaged chimney, replaced some broken blinds, checked the heating ducts and changed the air filters in the furnace.

I mean to tell you, extension of this episode-free time was a rarity for me. While I was in the middle of a stretch of depression, the extremes stayed balanced during my stay with Adam. I never knew when my mood was going to plunge, so I took advantage of every moment we had together.

After a few other minor repairs and some cleaning, we got to the fun part. Shopping! At the furniture outlet down the street, Adam found a nice, barely used couch and coffee table for his living room as well as some other small pieces he liked. We bought and installed a new refrigerator and snapped up a lawnmower on sale at the end of the season.

Adam started his teaching job while I stuck around to do some work on the yard. I loved working with my hands, especially outdoors! With my illness in check for the moment, I tackled the task. It filled me with joy and a sense of fulfillment to be able to help Adam by mowing his lawn. I had never stopped cutting my own grass through the years of mental anguish. Though, sometimes, I had to push myself through depression to keep going. In fact, there were times when I cut the front yard one day and the back yard the next.

I wondered how long this season of good energy would last. Dare I hope for more than what I had right now?

The answer came soon and in a manner I couldn't have expected in my lifetime. As we finished up at the bank, opening an account for Adam, the lobby went silent and every eye turned toward the television screen sitting in the corner of the waiting area. Horror glazed over the faces of those watching as the twin towers crumbled. Gasps erupted in small pockets around the room. Most of us just stared in disbelief. A terrorist bombing? In the United States of America?

As we witnessed the unfolding events, people running from the scene, falling or jumping from the shattered buildings, soot scattering itself throughout a several block radius, I recognized the answer to my question.

All we have is today. Right now. The present. With all its insecurities, its defects, its wonders. It has little to do with lingering in the struggles of pain and everything to do with seizing the moments of life as they come, whatever their packaging. They are fleeting. Not one of us knows what moment will be our last.

The tragedy unfolding in New York City and later in Pennsylvania unleashed for me a renewed appreciation for my family, especially, that day, for my son Adam. He was embarking on a new adventure separate from the household he grew up in. He would be making his way in much the same manner as I did when I left home for the first time. But this season would be different for us than it was for my dad and me. I wanted a relationship with my son. He wanted a relationship with his dad. Together, we determined to stay connected.

Adam settled in well with his life in North Carolina. Linda and I were so proud of him. Setting up a household of his own wasn't easy. But he gave himself to the process and to the ways God grew him through it. He started with only sixteen guitar students. With the income generated from those lessons, he could barely eek by with the essentials of rent and his utility bills. The house was difficult to heat in the fall and winter with such high ceilings and no insulation. In the summertime, cooling the house down seemed next to impossible. In addition, Adam needed to keep his car gassed for the commute from Wake Forest to Raleigh, and he needed to buy food.

Building up his list of students became important. But Adam's need to live meagerly built a relationship with God that grew into his first priority. He began to rely on God in ways he hadn't needed to before. His prayers came from a place of desperation. He submitted to God's "hammering," as he called it, and graciously received God's faithful provision in all areas of his life.

UNEXPECTED LIFELINE

Within a short time, Adam met and began dating a beautiful young lady. She worked near the music store and came in the afternoons for guitar lessons. With music, sweet spirits, and a love of adventure on a shoestring budget in common, she and Adam developed quite a friendship.

Only a few weeks after they began dating, Adam brought his friend home to meet the family and take in a day at the amusement park in Williamsburg. Linda and I really liked this girl. She seemed a good fit for Adam, sensible, hardworking, and beautiful inside and out.

Just before Christmas, Adam called to see whether we still had my mother's diamond ring. The ring was on consignment, but we were thrilled to make the trip to Richmond to retrieve it. We even had the jeweler clean and reset the stone so Adam would have a radiant treasure to give his girl when he was ready.

While Adam was home during his holiday break, he told us he planned to surprise his girlfriend with the ring and a proposal sometime in January. We were so excited for him, and for us! A daughter! We were gaining a daughter, and a precious one too.

That same Christmas, Adam's friend who had been studying in Oxford came to visit his family in Richmond over the Christmas break. Adam invited me to join him and Hank for lunch at the Penny Lane Pub. I loved spending time with Adam and looked forward to every minute. Having Hank there would be a perk, as would the English ale.

From the time we walked in as a trio, our fellowship went deep. Adam and I pelted Hank with theological questions, dying to know what it was like to study under the master theologians at Oxford. Hank engaged us in conversation about my bipolar disorder. He knew I struggled with extreme mood swings and suffered recently with severe depression. His comments and insights encouraged both Adam and me. "I'm astounded at your depth and desire for spiritual things," he said, "in spite of all the difficulties you endure. That you can still bear witness to the living Christ speaks volumes about the relationship you have with Him in spite of your illness."

Adam shot me a knowing look, filled with pride for his dad and tempered with a humble heart toward God. (He truly is an amazing young man. I'm blessed to be a part of his life; privileged to call him my son.)

Hank seemed to enjoy our time together. As we gathered our belongings to leave after our wonderful afternoon of conversation, he told us that no one else had spoken a word to him about the Scriptures since he had been back from England. Not even his family. We were stunned.

The New Year rang in, and Adam returned to North Carolina. Linda and I waited excitedly for him to call with the outcome of his marriage proposal. The call came, and Adam spilled the details of that special evening. She said yes and the ring fit!

Within a few months, the excitement died. Adam's intended returned the ring to him and said she didn't want to marry him after all. The news caught Adam off guard. While he recognized some issues in their relationship that would be difficult to resolve, he believed they would be able to work through them with commitment and hard work. She didn't agree.

Broken, though not devastated, Adam went back to life without her in it. Since he lived alone and had been courting for a while, her absence affected him more than he thought it would. He missed her friendship. Feelings of loneliness and isolation began to grow. He was used to going out with her two or three times a week. Adam hadn't focused on making a lot of friends outside of their relationship. He knew only a few other people at the new church he attended and a couple of guys from work.

But through this trying season of isolation and heartache, God began doing a deep work in Adam, growing him in humility and calling for his attention. The Holy Spirit seemed to be taking him to a place of total surrender. He dug even deeper into books by Francis Schaeffer, C. S. Lewis, and other theologians. These men of God, profound thinkers of their day, infused Adam's mind with truth.

Adam also explored books of prayers and devotions and listened to music that would challenge and strengthen him spiritually. He became so centered in Christ that he considered adopting a cloistered lifestyle. After a season of intense prayer and a great deal of research, particularly with the Brothers and Sisters of Charity at Little Portion Hermitage in Georgia, he decided that wasn't for him. But the process took him deeper into relationship with Jesus than anyone I've ever known.

Our Sunday afternoon phone conversations often extended into the evening as we discussed the Scriptures and all that the Lord was teaching us. We shared our struggles and concerns, and I kept him up to speed with what was happening with my mental illness. Some weeks I had great victories to report. Other weeks I needed extra prayer as I sloshed through every pitch of darkness.

Whatever direction the discussion turned, Adam always encouraged me. He earnestly prayed for my healing, calling for the Lord to release me from the shackles of disease. He had experienced, firsthand, the profound effect of Christ on my life in his growing-up years. He knew the fire in me for God long before I was struck with this dreaded illness. Adam prayed with me for complete restoration and a fanning of the flame that once burned with a passion to serve the Lord.

My son amazed me. He helped me believe that it could happen. He gave me hope that my life could be rich and full again, not just lived in the gaps or the in between places. We spiritually encouraged and sharpened each other, fulfilling the passage in Proverbs 27:17 that says, "As iron sharpens iron, so one man sharpens another." Recalling the depth and power of our relationship at that time still moves me.

At twenty-five years old, Adam challenged me to hold on to Jesus, to hang in there spiritually, even when I would never understand the breadth of bipolar disorder or have a clue why it happened to me.

Adam carried wisdom from the Lord and a maturity way beyond his years.

As the enemy pressed in, laying siege to every part of my life for twelve years, Adam became my lifeline. Unexpected and true. Grace filled and strong. He constantly pointed me toward Scripture and back into relationship with the God who loves me, no matter what. He dedicated his life, his time, his talents to God. That impacted me. His passion to center on God and not himself turned my life around.

Adam was intentional with the students he was privileged to teach. Nothing he did was by accident. Everything he did was a calling, even teaching guitar at a seemingly random store in the middle of Raleigh. He knew he was positioned for "such a time as this" (Esther 4:14) to be an influence on those who came to be taught.

He challenged me to stay engaged with my life. Though I continued to be tormented with repeated thoughts of suicide and even homicide, Adam reassured me that God would not let me go. He anchored me in the midst of my storm so I wouldn't drift so far out to sea I could never return. Adam was, and is, a man above men. My counselor. My mentor. My son.

Because of Adam's influence, I held on to the truth of God's all-knowing, sovereign hand of protection in my life. Adam showed me the truth of R. C. Sproul's statement: "God doesn't just throw a life preserver to a drowning person. He goes to the bottom of the sea, and pulls a corpse from the bottom of the sea, takes him up on the bank, breathes into him the breath of life and makes him alive."

At times, like the short season of getting Adam moved into his new home, I recognized the breath of life and knew myself to be among the living. Other times, I found myself lying on the bank, limp and breathless, certain I wanted to die. Then I would hear Adam's voice on the other end of the phone line, pleading, loving, strong: "Dad, hold on. Hold on, Dad. Just hold on. I'm on my way. I'm coming home."

CHAPTER 11

A LIFESAVING ENCOUNTER

Without God, man has no reference point to define himself.
—R. C. Sproul

In spite of the influences of my sons, my wife, and others, the enemy seemed intent to pull me under and keep me under. Depression hit me hard and for extended periods of time. Every episode took me further into stifling darkness. I was suffocating.

I did what every strong man does; I tried harder. Just like when I was a kid. Exercise became a way for me to manage my problems. I suppose it made me feel as though I still maintained some control in my life, at least over my own body. I was determined to do everything I could to combat the depression.

Being a disciplined person, I started early in the morning with sit-ups, crunches, and leg lifts. Not just a few of each, nor the hundreds I could do during the mania, but I pushed myself to do as many as I could do. Then I rode my bike several miles down the road. And when I got back, I dropped to the floor for a string of push-ups. The neighbors stared at me every time I went outside, but I didn't care. I was battling against all odds, desperate to keep my life going.

On coherent days, I knew I had a good life with an amazing family. On bad days, my life and I were estranged. Separated by an unexplainable black hole. I couldn't sit back and let it consume every good thing. I did what I could to push back the edges that seemed to be closing in on me. But nothing worked. Not one thing. No matter how hard I fought, the episodes came; triggered by nothing evident to me or to the doctors or to my family. They were random events, dark and discouraging random events.

I found myself giving into the darkness. I was surrounded by it. I slept in it. Ate in it. Walked in it. Sat in it. Waited in it. It was all I could do. I waited for it to pass. Waited for my life to return. I grew tired of waiting. Waiting in the dark is a lonely, debilitating life.

I tried praying, quietly at first. Then I fervently prayed in the name of Jesus to rebuke the enemy as this torment threatened.

The episodes of darkness escalated.

GOD! Where are You? Why won't You do something? Why did You abandon me? Leave me here in the dark to die? Alone?

I sat in my darkness and watched God moving in everyone's life but my own. Linda began spending serious time with God in prayer and meditation. Through this strengthened relationship, she began having friends over for Bible study and fellowship. Not just cookies and coffee kind of fellowship but the real, deep kind. I mean to tell you, those women prayed and supported each other. Some days I had to leave because my spirit was in such conflict with the presence of the Spirit in the house.

Adam's encounters with God also struck me as profound. He saw God everywhere he went. And out of the overflow of his time with God, Adam impacted the people around him. I knew Linda and Adam both prayed for me. I knew they enlisted others to pray for me. Even people I had never met prayed for me.

How could God stand by and be so quiet with all these faithful Christians praying? I didn't understand His silence.

Silence, for me, had been a deliberate way of hiding from uncomfortable circumstances or people I wanted to avoid, even as a young

A LIFESAVING ENCOUNTER

child. Why would God want to hide Himself from me? Was I that repulsive? Or pathetic? Or hopeless?

Yes. Hopeless and getting worse. Dejected. Without God or my family, I had no hope. I had no identity outside of manic-depressive disorder. R. C. Sproul, another of my favorite authors, says, "Without God, man has no reference point to define himself." That, I understood. I had nothing. I was nothing. I deserved nothing.

I had done all I could do. The doctors had done all they could do. Linda had done all she could do. I was ready to be done. Done with God. Done with suffering. Done with life.

On Sunday afternoon, November 10, 2002, when Linda got home from church, I told her that I had had enough. Suicidal and homicidal thoughts plagued me again. I wasn't getting better. I was getting worse.

Linda shook her head and blurted out, "Only God can help you, now, Ray." I guess she was done too.

Later on that day, Adam and I connected for our regular Sunday afternoon phone call. As usual, he engaged me in a debate of the Scriptures and challenged me to continue on with my life. "Dad, you need to endure the suffering places you're walking through. Determine to yield to the Holy Spirit and fight with the faith God gave you."

I wanted to fight. Really, I did. I just didn't have much fight left.

I went to bed confused, battling to keep my thoughts clear so I could determine my next steps of action. In the chaos of my mind, I couldn't find the balance between yielding and fighting. They seemed contradictory. I decided to let them simply cancel each other out.

The next morning, Veteran's Day, I got up in pretty much the same state as I'd gone to bed. But I still went to Rockwood Park for my doubles tennis team court time. Playing sports had always been a good outlet. But although tennis had become my activity of choice, it grew harder and harder for me to focus on the ball.

The mind-altering side effects of the medications my mind required adversely affected my body. As usual during streaks of depression, I experienced difficulty on the court, stumbling and missing serve after serve. Though people tended to treat me with kindness and understanding, even bordering on pity, I was utterly humiliated. In my stubbornness, I determined to play through the frustration.

Residue from that humiliating match and from the dark cloud hanging over my head seemed to come out in every encounter of the day. I was confused and depressed, even dazed.

When I arrived home at my wit's end, I sat in my parked car to catch my breath before heading into the house. I knew what I needed. A walk.

I hurried into the house, snapped the leash on Sophie, and out the door we went. She was happy and carefree as a lark. Always smiling. Walking with Sophie always seemed to calm me down, reminding me of the days when I used to run with Freto after school. I never thought I'd consider those days carefree, but they were, compared to my current circumstances.

Sophie and I walked part of the way down the street and trotted back toward the house together. A sudden downpour whipped up, requiring that we pick up the pace. I hoped the run, even in the rain, would do me good. We were out of breath and both panting as we came in the door.

I could still feel the weight of the day, of my disorder. Depression loomed over me. The pleasured moments during my walk with Sophie fled. My rope was getting very short. I didn't have much left to hold on to. I could hear Adam's words in my mind: "Hold on, Dad. Just hold on."

Mercy, Lord Jesus. Have mercy.

Linda, knowing what an awful day it had been, fixed one of my favorite meals, baked chicken and string beans canned from our garden, with sweet tea to soothe my soul. As we sat down to eat together, I could barely tune in to a single word she shared. I missed our conversations. Since the first day we laid eyes on each other, Linda and I have been best friends. There were times throughout our life together that we could have talked for days straight through. But that night at the dinner table, I sat with mush for a brain, staring out the window. Zero frequency.

At the time, I was probably oblivious to the tension hanging over us in that awkward silence. Looking back on it, my heart aches. Linda was my life. My ally. My lover. My friend. She had endured so much, choosing to stay with me even when I begged her to go. The weight of the hurt I must have caused her seems unbearable to me even now. I would never be able to make it up to her. Never. Ever.

In the midst of our silence, as Linda cleared the table, I moved to the couch, hoping to relax. Instead, pressure mounted. Unanswerable questions poured into my brain. How long would my family be able to endure the siege this illness placed over our lives? Would I be haunted by this deplorable condition for the rest of my life?

I couldn't sit still in the middle of this maddening, one-sided conversation. I paced, shaking my fist at some invisible intruder and mumbling to myself something about insanity. If I could have flown to the moon in that moment, I would have. Freedom. I longed for it. An escape from wrestling with daily activities. A release from the weight of responsibility. To abandon the cares of the world for the ease of floating in space. Freedom. I wanted it. Any form of it. Now.

My pacing led me into the backyard. With a seven-foot-tall privacy fence running the perimeter, the yard had always been somewhat of a haven for Linda and me. The large contained area gave Sophie plenty of room to run and roll without getting out into the traffic. In the midsummer season, it had brimmed with life. Flower and vegetable gardens flourished. A maple tree and a poplar stood tall, offering colorful shade for those who wanted to linger under them. They held out their branches for young boys who wished to become famous explorers. I wondered whether my father would have been proud. I could still hear him telling my mother, "They're such good boys. Good boys."

On this November night the air was cool and free from the tiny flashes of lightening bugs that had been so plentiful in the summertime. Stars sparkled overhead in their constellations. I paused to soak in the beauty of this fall season, hoping it would transcend the darkness I felt in my spirit. I tipped back my head and fired questions toward the dwelling place of the unseen God. "Why did You abandon me? Leave me alone in the hours of my greatest need? I loved You. I served You. And this is my reward? Explain yourself. Tell me the purpose of this suffering."

Deafening silence hung in the air except for the voices that taunted me from the inside. *End it,* they whispered. *End it all.* An unbearable darkness consumed me to the very depths of my soul as I stepped down into the hot tub. *This must be how it feels to drown.* I resigned myself to death, stopped flailing, and made a move toward ending my misery. Naked and filled with shame, I let out one last desperate groan. "Oh, GOD! Please … have Your way with me!"

Without a second's gap, or an ounce of understanding, the supernatural power of the Almighty God came upon me.

I began weeping uncontrollably as He brought me to the point of full surrender. I cried out in searing agony, "Lord, forgive me. Save my life. Have mercy on me, a sinner. Release me from the entrapments of this battle. I can't live this way anymore." Peace flooded over me, as if I were standing in the middle of a fountain. "Mercy, Lord. More of Your mercy."

There I stood. Undone in the mercy of the Lord. I'd never before known a closeness with God like that night. My mind filled with songs, as if He were singing over me. I stood, tears flowing, basking in the glow of God's presence. I recalled a promise that, until November 11, 2002, I assumed was just words on a page, written to a different people in a different time: "Indeed we count them blessed who endure. You have heard of the perseverance of Job and seen the end intended by the Lord—that the Lord is very compassionate and merciful" (James 5:11 NKJV).

A LIFESAVING ENCOUNTER

Praise You, Lord. Thank You for Your nearness to me, even in my terrible state of brokenness.

Linda. Oh, my Linda!

I snagged my clothes and went in to find my bride. I felt like a young man, meeting the woman who would become his wife for the very first time. There she stood in the kitchen, putting the last of the dishes in an overhead cabinet. I caught her unaware, slid my arms around her waist and pulled her toward me.

My tears fell as she turned around to face me. "Oh, Linda …" I got all choked up and could hardly speak. "I am so sorry. … I know I've hurt you. Please … forgive me?"

"Ray?"

"Yes, it's me. Really me. Ray Sturt. I'm the man you married, and I love you."

Linda stood in disbelief. It had been twelve long years since I had spoken these precious words to her. She had been my anchor, steadfast and resolute. Rarely wavering. Leaning only on the Lord as her provider, her comforter, her everything. I had been nothing but thoughtless. A weight around her neck. I didn't mean to be. But I know I was. And here I stood in front of her, changed, only by the healing hand of our merciful God.

I could see the question in her eyes. She wanted to believe, but did she dare? She hugged me.

"Is this for real? What happened to you out there?"

As I shared my profound God encounter with Linda, her eyes began to dance.

"Ray, God heard our prayers! It's a miracle!"

Like the one leper who returned to give Jesus thanks when he saw that he was healed (see Luke 17), we went immediately to the Lord to offer Him our thanksgiving. I put our favorite cassette into the tape player, and we worshiped for hours, singing and raising our hands in spontaneous praise. What a wonderful, God-ordained, beautiful night!

When God touches your life in a real and mighty way, it's just not possible to keep quiet.

✦

Settling in beside Linda when we got to church the next Sunday, I began to recognize the amazing gift I'd been given. We sat together where Linda had been sitting alone for nearly twelve years. Tears welled up in my eyes. Linda had held on when I couldn't. Faithfully sitting here, seeking the Lord's intervention on my behalf, receiving her suffering as a gift, all the while loving me when I couldn't love her back. I'm grateful for a wife who loves the way Jesus loves. I slipped my hand in Linda's and gave it a knowing squeeze.

Tears welled up in my eyes. God showered such compassion and power on me, I couldn't contain my grateful heart.

The worship leader stepped to the platform, and we rose to our feet. I soaked in the words of each song. We sang old hymns I hadn't heard in years. As the message was delivered, the Scriptures came alive for me once again, igniting my spirit with new fire from above.

The enemy had laid siege to every aspect of my life, shaking my faith and filling me with doubt for too many years. While every good thing seemed to have been cut off from me, I knew that God hadn't let me go and that He still loved me. I just couldn't always see evidence of it with my manic-depressive mind so full of enemy lies and warfare.

I prayed that I would be able to manage the responsibilities that go along with knowing the healing hand of God. Not just singing about being grateful, but living it.

✦

A week after my lifesaving encounter in the hot tub with God, Linda and I sat at the dinner table, sharing thoughts about the whole experience and my response to it. "I have such peace of mind now," I announced. "I'm sleeping well and nearly functioning like my old self again."

A LIFESAVING ENCOUNTER

After twelve years of torture and hell, I was amazed at how well I was doing. But I felt a little unsure how to respond to this new me. Could this healing really be complete?

"I've had good days before and always knew that they weren't going to last," I said. "The threat of this being part of the extremes scares me, Linda. But if I can temper my excitement and keep a leash on my sadness, then maybe I'll be able to pull this off."

"Ray, you are no more in control of your life now than you were a week ago. God was just as sovereign then as He is now. He did a beautiful and gracious thing for you. For us. Let's be glad for it and believe it to be complete. Just because you don't have bipolar illness anymore doesn't mean that God's work in you is done."

The realization that I was no longer bipolar caught me unaware. Unaware, until now, that I held within me, not only a resurrected life in the spiritual sense, but also a body and mind fully restored by the power of Almighty God. Like the leper, I walked away from my lifesaving encounter knowing forgiveness through the grace of God. But I didn't know that I'd been healed! Not completely.

I had become so used to reacting to the random displays of chaos in my brain that I hadn't allowed myself full awareness of the depth of peace now permeating my spirit. Or of the profound conversations I enjoyed without anxiety and confusion. Or of the light pouring through the clouds of despair that had loomed over my days.

Linda's eyes widened. Something turned on like a light bulb in her head. Her reassuring voice broke through my thoughts.

"I think you should stop taking your medications." I put down my fork and looked straight in her face.

"But you know what happens when I miss my meds. I can't live without them. No."

Desperation had led me to do some crazy things with my medications behind my doctor's back. It didn't go well. Manic episodes always drove me back to taking my pills. All of them. I finally accepted my dependence and acknowledged that I needed help to manage my life. Without the meds, I was totally out of control. Distraught. Lost. No matter how good I felt, a shift could occur in a split second.

Fear welled up in me. Just the thought of the risk tested me. "Experience was my teacher, Linda. I can't mess with the meds."

"Well, Ray, all you can do is put it to the test. See for yourself what will happen. Prove it. See if the battle returns."

Linda made a good point. God healed me. Completely. If I no longer had bipolar disease, I no longer needed the bipolar meds. That day I put my life in God's hands, allowed Him to conquer my fear, and discontinued every psychiatric medication. I haven't taken one pill since. "What is impossible with men is possible with God" (Luke 18:27).

Over the coming days, I explored life as a free man. A new man. No longer bound by the label of bipolar disorder, but released from the snares of my adversary to proclaim sweet victory in the name of Jesus. Victory over the disorder and victory in life.

One of the sweetest spoils of this life-sustaining victory was falling in love with my Linda all over again. God used the fertile ground of our difficulties to grow us. He restored our marriage and refueled our passion for Him and for each other.

Consider a beautiful garden being destroyed and lying vacant with no hope of life or the ability to sustain it. For twelve years Linda sat in the middle of that lifeless garden, caring for the soil and praying for its protection. She guarded it the best she could from intruders and from the many storms passing through. She saw life and beauty no one else could see.

Looking back and seeing that garden through Linda's eyes helps me see things the way God sees them. Out of what the enemy intended for destruction, God raised up new life. A life radically changed in one, merciful, unexplainable moment—what a precious gift, this miracle of life. I gave myself to it.

Yes, I surrendered. Not to the enemy bipolar disorder but to the true life given to me in Christ. The siege was over.

Undeserving and grateful, I began to take back everything I knew and loved, one day at a time.

A LIFESAVING ENCOUNTER

I started with Linda, becoming more aware of the depth and beauty she carried so humbly. Some mornings, before she even brushed her hair, she simply took my breath away. Before the illness took over our lives, we loved each other, without doubt. We even liked each other quite well and enjoyed spending time together. But since we received this precious gift from God, we take nothing for granted.

I am now more aware to honor Linda as the one and only love of my life. I hold doors open for her and listen with a tuned-in ear to every word she expresses. She speaks so calmly that when she's finished, her gentle, flowing words still linger in my mind.

Even after twelve years, we remembered the joys of sharing what we have in common, like reading together, having devotions, and listening to our favorite Christian CDs every morning while eating breakfast. We worked outside in the garden or did yard work or played tennis. In the evenings, we sat in the family room together as Linda read to me, or we watched television. We enjoyed documentaries, a few romantic comedies, and we especially liked keeping up with the sports world. Every now and then, I could talk Linda into watching a good old-fashioned western with me. In my book, you can't beat John Wayne for manly entertainment!

With my patience and strength restored, I could play tennis again with accuracy, defeating my opponents with ease. I could drive anywhere I needed to go without having any near tragedies. And I helped Linda again by sharing in our household duties.

Where paranoia once threatened and caused me to withdraw from people, God gave me a keen awareness of those He placed around me. Being with people now brought me great joy. Every day was like a mission to discover who God was sending across my path. I see all people for their uniqueness and worth as God created them in His image and for His glory.

From my despicable heart, God restored a desire to imitate Christ by loving and serving my fellow man. "Your attitude should be the same as that of Christ Jesus: Who, being in very nature God, did not consider equality with God something to be grasped, but made himself nothing, taking the very nature of a servant, being made in human likeness" (Phil. 2:5–7).

The power of Christ in me restored allows me to love in ways I wouldn't have dreamed of loving during my illness. In fact, when I was sick, my family and I could have used a measure of human kindness and understanding. I didn't moan over it at the time, and I don't stew about what could have been different if only people had reached out. But coming through a season of being an outcast gave me an extra awareness and sensitivity I wouldn't have otherwise. Every one of us deserves to be acknowledged, affirmed, and loved just the way we are, even with our weaknesses and abnormalities. There are people all around waiting to be blessed by those willing to love like Jesus loved in simple ways, throughout everyday life.

With St. Francis of Assisi, let my prayer be, "Lord, make me an instrument of Your peace; where there is hatred, let me sow love; where there is injury, pardon; where there is doubt, faith; where there is despair, hope; where there is darkness, light; and where there is sadness, joy."

And where there is death, life. Surrendered and strong in the name of Jesus. A life worth celebrating.

CHAPTER 12

SUFFERING ENDURED

A hero is an ordinary individual who finds the strength to persevere and endure in spite of overwhelming obstacles.
—Christopher Reeve

Every echo of our celebration came to a screeching halt just thirty-two days after my healing with a phone call from Scott's boss. Through tears of hysterics, he tried to tell me about a horrific accident at the sawmill. "I put Scott in my truck ... took him to the medical center in Chester ... they sedated him and put him in an ambulance ... he's at the Medical College of Virginia Hospital ... in the trauma ER."

Scott was in serious trouble. I thanked Mr. Wells for his call and immediately called Linda, who was out Christmas shopping. I grabbed Scott's power-of-attorney papers, and we set out toward Richmond within the hour. We had no idea what sort of trauma Scott endured. But he would receive excellent care at the Virginia Hospital, a teaching institution known for its exceptional ability to respond to patients needing special procedures. The half-hour drive seemed to take an eternity.

Uncertainty flooded our minds and began to fill our conversation. We didn't want to give the enemy a minute, because he would certainly demand the day. So right then and there, we determined to praise God and to keep praising God, no matter what.

BIPOLAR VICTORY

Along the way we called Adam to enlist him as a prayer warrior. He joined in our praise and encouraged us with Scripture: "In every thing give thanks: for this is the will of God in Christ Jesus concerning you" (1 Thess. 5:18 KJV).

Linda also called a friend from her Bible study group, asking her to pray and to contact the other ladies. Engaging our community in the middle of our battle strengthened us for the hours that lie ahead, hours that began with prayers and worship through our tears.

Nurses met us at the front desk in the ER and ushered us to where Scott lie in shock. Pale and even grayish in appearance, his skin told the tale of a trauma resulting in lots of lost blood. A large blood-soaked gauze bandaged his right hand. Dried blood covered his shirt and jeans. In spite of what we saw, Linda and I both cried tears of relief. Scott recognized us and even responded to some of our questions.

He had cut off all four fingers from his right hand on a lumber saw and nearly severed his thumb too. His boss quickly gathered the fingers and placed them in a clean container on ice. The thought made me shudder, but I felt grateful for all this man had done for Scott.

"You know what today is, don't you?" Scott's nurse asked us, as if she were uncomfortable with the quiet of our waiting. "It's Friday the thirteenth! Some luck, huh?"

Immediately I raised my hands in the air and proclaimed truth over the lies of the enemy. "This is the day which the LORD hath made; we will rejoice and be glad in it" (Ps. 118:24 KJV).

Battling the enemy requires continual engagement. God brought healing and victory in the midst of my personal struggles against bipolar disorder, but the enemy continued to pound away at the Sturt family. I knew the darkness and did all I could to equip myself against it by walking closely with the Lord. Through the power of His Word and in the strength of His fellowship, the Sturts would face the challenges before us.

"Mr. and Mrs. Sturt?" One of the surgeons stepped into the room, introduced himself, and began to inform us that Scott would be

SUFFERING ENDURED

undergoing lengthy, microscopic hand surgery to reattach his damaged fingers.

"Will he be able to play the viola again?" Linda asked. "He plays with the Petersburg Symphony Orchestra. I can't imagine how hard it would be on him to never play again."

The doctor assured us that they would go the extra mile to insure a successful surgery—a surgery that would take him and his team, operating in shifts, a minimum of nine hours to complete.

Within minutes, an attendant came to wheel Scott to the operating room. We said our good-byes and headed out, certain that we would feel less anxious at home than sitting at the hospital the whole time.

On the drive home, I sensed apprehension in Linda's voice as she expressed concern for Scott's well-being. Finally, she blurted out, "Why did the county have to place him in such a dangerous job? They knew his history of mental illness."

"Scott loves his work at the lumber yard," I said, "and his supervisor always has high praise for his abilities. We don't know what caused Scott's accident or how it happened. Trying to figure things out or find a place for blame will do us no good whatsoever." I reached for Linda's hand. "Let's be grateful for Scott's life and leave him in God's hands, okay? God knows his needs far better than we do. Every one of them."

Linda nodded in agreement and started a conversation with God that carried us the rest of the way home. Even in her exhaustion, she prayed with vulnerability and strength. My Linda. What a gift.

Around midnight, the phone quickly jarred us back to reality from our dazed state of sleeplessness. Neither of us could rest. Linda read various Scripture passages to soothe our minds while we waited for some news. The voice on the other end announced that Scott came through his surgery well and would be in the recovery room for another few hours.

I saw the relief in Linda's eyes as she repeated the doctor's words. "Scott came through the surgery well."

Then the doctor took a deep breath and let it out slowly. Linda braced herself for the news to come. "We worked really hard as a team to reattach Scott's fingers. We did all we could, but the fingers were just too mangled to save. I'm so sorry."

"We managed to repair Scott's thumb, and we think it will be okay. His little finger only has a small stub left. We were also able to reattach his middle finger, so he'll be able to grasp things. But we can't guarantee that it will survive. If not, it will need to be removed."

The doctor went on to say that Scott would be sedated throughout the night as he began the long process of recovery.

I ached for my son. He had suffered so much in his twenty-nine years. Labeled with a learning disability in the third grade, none of his teachers thought he would ever be able to achieve much. But he beat the odds and gained acceptance into the music program at Shenandoah University after graduating high school. He lived to play the viola for the glory of God. But manic-depressive disorder stole away his dreams and cut his college career short in the middle of his sophomore year. It devastated him. It devastated me.

This darkness hovering over Scott came through my bloodline. In the middle of a dreadful season myself at the time, I didn't want to believe it. My bright-eyed son, Scott Sturt. Bipolar. Unbearable, but true.

I battled against the enemy the night of Scott's accident, hearing loudly the lie of blame. I wondered for a moment why God touched me with His healing hand, and not Scott. By the grace of God, I recognized the deceit and came against it with the power of His Word. A Scripture that the enemy once used against me now came back for me to use against him. "And we know that in all things God works for the good of those who love him, who have been called according to his purpose" (Rom. 8:28).

Praise You, God, for in Your sovereignty You know the purpose to which Scott has been called. Protect him. Strengthen him. Help him to endure. Heal him. He belongs to You. Continue to use him for Your glory.

After the initial shock of seeing Scott hooked up with IV lines and a morphine pump as well as other medical necessities, Linda and I settled into a grateful spirit. Scott needed our help to do just about everything, from bathing to shaving and even eating. We acknowledged his injury and loved Scott for the strong, capable man he is. Adapting to life without fingers on his right hand would be a challenge, but we were prepared to walk with him in the hard places, keeping our eyes fixed "on Jesus, the author and perfecter of our faith" (Heb. 12:2).

Within a week following the initial surgery, Scott suffered a setback. In spite of all the efforts of the doctors, including the use of leeches to stimulate circulation, the infusion of high-powered antibiotics, and our fervent prayers, the plastic surgeon took Scott back into surgery to remove the transplanted finger. I wondered whether Scott would ever find anything as fulfilling for him as playing the viola. *Mercy, Lord Jesus. Have mercy.*

People from Scott's church rallied around him with support that really lifted his spirits. They stopped by to visit and to pray, often bringing gifts to warm up an otherwise sterile hospital room. It soon looked like a floral shop! Linda took care to set the numerous cards where Scott could enjoy them. Some wrote in words of affirmation and healing. Through these gestures we observed Scott's community in action. They loved him. And he responded with a growing strength that encouraged his mother and me. One woman came in and set up a little Christmas tree for us all to enjoy, just like my mom had done for me.

And the pastor, whom Scott adored, came bearing an extra-special gift—an article he had downloaded from the Internet that told the stories of several young violinists, each with a prosthetic right hand. Somehow, even with their limiting physical condition, they all still played! The article included a photograph showing every one of those players with their instruments under their chins. What a beautiful thing this pastor did for Scott, offering him the gift of hope. If these kids could play, so could he. Scott beamed to think that he might once again play the viola or accompany his pastor on the guitar for worship.

Under the care of excellent physicians and by the grace of God, Scott remained in the hospital for a mere eleven days following his complicated and extensive surgeries. On December 24, 2002, we brought him home for an amazing Christmas together with Adam, as a family. The Lord gifted us with so much life. What a joyful time of celebration.

Once the new year rolled around, so too did Scott's new life. It tested his endurance. It tested my endurance. But we continued to put our faith in God, trusting Him for our every need.

With Scott's hand therapist located in Richmond at the Nelson Hand Clinic, I became Scott's chauffeur. The time in the car gave us opportunity to talk about the challenges he faced. Days before the accident, his mother and I watched him struggle through days of extreme irritation, snapping at Sophie and complaining of constant physical pain. When we pressed him, he admitted that he had stopped taking all of his bipolar medications. "I'm fine, Dad," he had said. He wasn't fine.

Eventually he agreed to go back on his meds. His mental-health coordinator required that he make an appointment with his doctor, which he did. By the time his appointment came up, he was completely wrung out. So depressed that he hadn't showered in days and could barely mutter a word to the doctor. My boy. He needed me to help him pay attention to his body and keep his mind alert. To help him be aware of how the enemy taunts those who suffer with bipolar illness.

SUFFERING ENDURED

Sometimes on the drives to Richmond, we memorized Scripture and listened to music. We still held hope that one day he would be able to play again.

Scott's top-notch hand therapist treated him using steaming whirlpools, massages, and painful hand exercises. He endured them with courage and great stamina, keeping in mind his goal of playing the viola. Only once did Scott come out of therapy and ask, "Did you hear me hollering? Ooooh, man, the pain!" Proud of Scott's determination and accomplishments, I felt sure that God would use this season for His glory, and I looked forward to watching Scott's progress.

In the meantime, on the days when I waited for Scott to finish his therapy sessions, God grew me in faith, endurance, and purpose. I took Scriptures on note cards to read and watched for opportunities to engage with people. During the siege bipolar disorder held on my life, relationships were taken away. I couldn't manage my own needs or pay attention to my family, let alone be aware of strangers. But God returned my joy of meeting new people ten times over.

"What are you reading?" a young woman asked as she walked past me in the clinic's waiting room. I showed her the Scripture on my card. "Therefore we do not lose heart. Even though our outward man is perishing, yet the inward man is being renewed day by day" (2 Cor. 4:16). She nodded politely and went on to share with me a few sentences of her discouragement. I handed her my Scripture card along with a message card entitled "Leave All Your Tangles to God."

Our paths crossed again a couple of weeks later. "Hey, you're the guy from the waiting room at the clinic, aren't you? I needed the encouraging words you shared with me that day. I even started going to church!" We talked for a while about her experience, and I shared with her from a gospel tract.

"Do you understand the difference between a 'saved sinner' and a 'lost sinner'?" I asked.

"I'm a 'lost sinner,'" she replied.

I could sense the Spirit of the Lord drawing her in as she earnestly sought to know the truth. "The Bible tells us, 'For everyone who asks receives; he who seeks finds; and to him who knocks, the door will be opened' (Matt. 7:8). So keep seeking God with all your heart."

This lady needed what she saw in me, though she may not have been able to put her finger on it: the presence of joy in spite of difficult circumstances. Her humble, open admission really moved my spirit. As we parted ways, I demonstrated Christian love with a hug. Not everyone would be comfortable with that, but she needed other human beings to reach beyond their comfort zones to express worthiness and love. I continued praying that she would not lose heart but would trust in the power of God to restore and raise up life from dry, brittle ground.

Scott endured this intensive hand therapy for seven weeks and three days. At the end of that time, his therapist encouraged us by saying that Scott healed faster than any other patient treated at the Nelson Hand Clinic with an injury as severe as he had sustained. Once again, with prayerful support from friends scattered in various parts of the country, Scott rose to the challenge set before him. He took the encouragement and benefits of his hard work home with him. He learned to change his bandages every day and managed to keep up with various exercises to strengthen his hand. His recovery seemed on a good course.

For a while after Scott went home, his mom and I stopped by his place frequently to help him transition into taking care of himself. With his hand still in heavy bandages, he needed some extra help. One morning I found something in his room that left me more than a little concerned. I called for Linda. "Look here behind the door. What do you make of that?"

Linda gasped as her eyes settled in on a huge hole in the wall, down close to the floor.

"Scott, son, come in here." I pointed. "How did this hole get here?"

Scott's eyes got real big. Then he started in describing a terrible scene. "Oh, man. She came at me, taunting me over and over with her horrifying accusations. I kicked at her to get rid of her mocking. It was awful. She wouldn't stop!"

As Scott flung his arms, mimicking the event he described, Linda's perception kicked in. "What happened to your hand? Where did all those bruises and scratches come from?" His left hand—no, not his "good" hand—looked swollen and damaged.

"Oh, yeah, well, I hit it on the door frame in the bathroom."

Finally we got the message. Scott was hallucinating. His face grew dark, shrouded again with the look of depression. He withdrew and went to his room to lie down. Moments later we heard his anger burst again. "Stop! Stop them!" he begged, sobbing uncontrollably, his head banging in response against the headboard. "Stop them! Stop!"

My heart broke. I know the edge of anger that erupts when you can't discern what's real and what isn't. Depression took its toll. Scott's accident left him full of anger and anguish in his soul. Losing his fingers hit him harder than his mother or I knew how to handle. I comforted him the only way I could in the moment. "We'll get through this, Scott. You're not alone. Ever."

Bipolar disorder sometimes behaves like a sniper, hiding and dropping down unexpectedly, requiring us to be aware and waiting, ready to respond when it makes a move. It's not a fight for the faint of heart. These episodes with Scott baffled us at times and challenged our endurance.

Like a siege, bipolar disorder threatened our family for years, finally running its course because we refused to give in. But the battle continues. An enemy either fights or forfeits. He doesn't just walk off the field. He simply chooses another angle. The attacks can be relentless. And as in the jungles of Vietnam, our enemy will ambush us. We needed to be prepared. We needed to prepare Scott. We were his allies, just as he and Adam and Linda were (and still are) mine.

We contacted his doctor right away, and that afternoon, January 17, 2003, we admitted Scott to a psychiatric facility for treatment. During his intake interview with the emergency room nurse, he acknowledged that he had not been taking his medications as prescribed by the doctor.

After a short stay in the hospital and getting back on all his meds, Scott emerged to see things in a whole new way. Determined and ready to receive more fully the life he'd been given, he began his journey back to independence. He started driving himself places, taking care of his household, and tying his own shoes. He even learned to write again, steadying the pen with his right thumb and what was left of his pinky finger. Every new thing he picked up spurred him toward conquering the next thing.

Above all, though, he wanted to play the viola. Finally, he had the confidence after his hand completely healed to try. To his amazement, grasping the bow between the thumb and pinky nub of his right hand, he could play. It took extra strength in his wrist, and after only minutes of playing, he began to complain of cramps in his hand.

The hand therapist at the clinic recommended a Richmond prosthetics and orthotics company. In July, I took Scott for his first appointment. The specialist first tried a glove-type prosthetic. This turned out to be purely cosmetic and allowed no movement whatsoever.

Following months of research and testing, experts came up with a plastic sheath molded to fit over Scott's right hand. It includes a mechanical joint and attaches permanently to the end of his bow with a metal fastener and a few screws. Held firmly in place with a Velcro strap across the back of his hand, this amazing contraption allows Scott to make a full range of sweeping wrist movements. In no time at all, he began playing the music we longed to hear.

And within weeks, he rejoined his pastor on stage with his viola for Sunday morning worship. The small country church folk rejoiced and

SUFFERING ENDURED

offered to God their thanksgiving for Scott's care and provision. Scott beamed. It had only been a year since his accident. But he gave himself to the life he'd been given and lived it. He loved nothing more than to glorify God with this special gift.

Scott continued on his path to recovery, not just by overcoming the interruptions of his hand injury or the bipolar episodes, but by being obedient to his calling in spite of the obstacles he faced. In January he returned to play for the Petersburg Symphony Orchestra.

We were all thrilled, of course, but perhaps none more than the symphony organization itself. Word spread throughout the community of Scott's amazing recovery and his miraculous return to the viola section. He created such a stir that the local newspaper featured a five-column story with the headline "Viola Player Returns to Symphony after Hand Injury." What do you think about that? Scott Sturt. My son, a local phenomenon.

With all the wonder surrounding Scott's recovery, to remember that the life he now lives grew from the fertile ground of suffering might seem a stretch to some. But not to us, and certainly not to Scott. He learned endurance in that fertile field. And he learned to trust. Just as his mother and I did. Just as his brother did. Not as one in the world would trust in himself, but as one who trusts His heavenly Father.

CHAPTER 13

EVERLASTING VICTORY

I have been all things unholy. If God can work through me, He can work through anyone.
—St. Francis of Assisi

I marvel at the way God preserved my sons in spite of the environment they endured in my household. I see the influence of their mother. Her steadfastness, her courage, her strength to rise in response to the Lord. Our boys are the men they are today in part because of what God did in and through her, and so am I.

God didn't make us to walk alone on this earth. He made us to be in relationship, loving Him and loving each other. Matthew 22 tells us that an expert of the law asked, "Teacher, which is the greatest commandment in the Law?" And Jesus answered, "'Love the Lord your God with all your heart and with all your soul and with all your mind.' This is the first and greatest commandment. And the second is like it: 'Love your neighbor as yourself'" (Matt. 22:36–39).

Let me tell you, loving God "with all your mind" becomes rather difficult when your mind belongs to a malady like bipolar disorder. And it's hard to love your neighbors if, when you come outside, they all go inside and lock their doors.

The extreme behaviors I experienced pushed every relationship away, and isolation took their place. Abandonment issues shot straight for the surface and stirred up all kinds of trouble. Maybe it happens for you that way too. I'll tell you, some days my moods seemed to have been on steroids! Isolation hit me hard and left me vulnerable to the enemy.

He set up snares and relentlessly pressed against me until he weakened my defenses. But I wouldn't give up, and neither would my family. Without warning, he surrounded me and cut off everything that sustained life, including my family, my job, my friends, and my faith. I was under siege.

The word *siege* actually comes from the Latin term *sedere,* which literally means "to sit." When an attacker encounters a fortress that can't be easily taken in a single surprise attack, he surrounds his target, blocks the escape of troops and the provision of supplies, and then waits. He sits, and he waits. What is he waiting for? Surrender.

A siege lasts until one or the other side surrenders. Gives in. Throws in the towel. Sometimes a military intervention occurs once a siege begins, but not often. With all of the access points sealed off, surrender always comes, whether because of starvation, or thirst, or disease.

After twelve grueling years under siege from bipolar episodes, I finally surrendered. Not to the syndrome or to my adversary, but to God and to the life I'd been given. It's the only surrender that actually gives life.

For me that includes the miraculous victory of physical healing, which strangely enough doesn't always feel like a gift. Virginia Woolf, spins an interesting perspective: "One likes people much better when they're beaten down by a prodigious siege of misfortune than when they triumph." Often when I talk about the miracle I received, people turn away, afraid to engage. They don't understand.

Miracles are mysterious. Sometimes the responsibility of a miraculous healing weighs on me. I want to hide in the quiet, but I can't. I'm called to be a light in the dark.

Guilt flashes at times as I wonder why I get to be healed but my son doesn't. Then I remember the sovereignty of God. I yield to Him the

EVERLASTING VICTORY

life I've been given, just as I am: chosen, called, forgiven. And healed, including His purposes for my healing.

And I yield to His purposes for Scott, who continues to suffer every single day under the siege of bipolar disorder. He would like nothing more than to be healed and often carries the burden of anger about his circumstances. He is growing as he learns to accept and manage the challenges of the life he's been given.

When the right time came for me to talk with Scott about my healing, I felt a bit apprehensive. But he surprised me with his wisdom. He looked me right in the eyes and said profoundly, "God has the right to do what He wants to do."

I was taken aback by the depth and truth of his statement. Who am I to question God?

As I walk in the wholeness of this miraculous, do-over life, being obedient to it as a calling in spite of the obstacles that come, God, in His grace, uses me. Not for my benefit but for the benefit of others and for His glory. What do you think about that? Me. Ray Sturt. Changed and used by God.

Now here's the kicker: you too can walk in the miraculous victory of a do-over life, no matter the obstacles you face. Yes, even if you're under the siege of bipolar disorder. As St. Francis of Assisi said, "I have been all things unholy. If God can work through me, He can work through anyone." To paraphrase the quote, "I have spit on the Word of God, walked out on my wife, nearly given in to a desperate illness. If God can work through me, Ray Sturt, He can work through anyone."

How would your paraphrase read? "I have squandered my life savings, threatened my neighbor's life, stood ready to jump from the edge of a tall building, and _____"? Fill in the blank, but remember there's more to your story.

The apostle Peter put it this way: "Those who suffer according to God's will should commit themselves to their faithful Creator and continue to do good" (1 Pet. 4:19).

One easygoing, summer afternoon, an old classmate of Linda's pulled up in our driveway. She lived seventy-five miles away, but she brought a friend of hers who had heard of my healing and seemed in desperate need of support.

When this precious lady stepped into our home, I could barely hold back my emotion. The conflict in her eyes, the weariness in her voice painted a picture of her battle. She began to cry. Depression kept her from being the anchor and support her family needed. Her family didn't have a clue how to be the anchor and support she needed.

Throughout our conversation, Bonnie honored us with her vulnerability. During a manic spending spree, she had depleted her savings account and charged thousands of dollars worth of clothing and household items at high-end specialty shops. She and her husband declared bankruptcy. "I was devastated. My husband didn't speak to me for weeks. I needed help, and I knew it. So I made an appointment with a psychologist. He told me that I likely suffered from bipolar disorder and would need an assortment of medications to balance out my extreme moods."

She became restless and hesitated for a minute. Then she continued. "That doctor didn't understand. My husband is disabled, and we have no insurance. We can't afford these kinds of medication. The Seroquel alone costs more than two thousand dollars for just a couple months' worth of pills! I'm at my rope's end. I don't know what to do."

Bonnie sat before us in utter dejection. We sat utterly amazed that God would bring this woman into our home where she could be accepted. Loved, not labeled. Encouraged, not judged.

Linda, with her very special way, moved to where Bonnie could see her face.

"Bonnie, you're not alone. You might feel abandoned, or even unworthy. But those are lies. A bipolar diagnosis doesn't have to send you into exile, and it doesn't mean that you aren't intelligent. Those are stigmas. Falsehoods. And sometimes they're perpetuated by unknowing loved ones, like me. When Ray got sick, I had a hard time accepting him at first. I still loved him. I just didn't understand the illness or know how to respond to his behaviors. In God's strength, I came around. But it took some time."

"I do feel alone," Bonnie said. "Even kind of stupid sometimes. Why did I have to go and buy all that stuff? ... I'm just already so tired."

My heart broke.

"I recognize that battle," I said. "The suffering and rejection are unimaginable. I couldn't have made it without Linda. I'm so grateful for the way God worked in her life and the way she responded. Your husband will come around too, with time and awareness, and grace. You'll help him from the strength of your own reliance on God. Remember that you are fearfully and wonderfully made by the Creator of the earth. Accept how He made you: with bipolar disorder. It's not a punishment. He's your heavenly Father, and He adores you. Trust Him. Believe Him. Know that you belong to Him."

"I want to trust and believe I am who He says I am," Bonnie responded. "I just don't want to be bipolar. Why do I have to be bipolar? Why can't God just heal me, Ray, like He did you?"

I can't answer that. Not for Bonnie. Not for my son Scott. Not for you. Maybe God will give you the victory of healing from bipolar disorder; He's the only one who knows. But there is something I do know. Victory can also be found outside of physical healing. It's the kind of victory that comes when you turn yourself toward God and trust Him completely for a grace-filled, abundant life, even in your suffering.

Several years ago, while Linda and I read aloud from *The Saturday Evening Post,* we discovered an article written by a professor of psychiatry at the Johns Hopkins School of Medicine. One of the foremost authorities on manic-depressive illness and coauthor of the standard medical text, Dr. Kay Redfield Jamison writes with wonder, passion, and knowledge. An intimate knowledge:

> Like millions of Americans, I was dealt a hand of intense emotions and volatile moods. I have had manic depressive illness, also known as bipolar disorder, since I was eighteen years old. It is an illness that ensures that those who have it will experience a frightening, chaotic and emotional ride. It is not a gentle or easy disease. And, yet, from it I have come to see how important a certain restlessness and discontent can be in one's life; how important the jagged edges and pain can be in determining the course and force of one's life.[4]

I couldn't believe what we were reading! This doctor suffers from the seige of bipolar disorder, yet she sits at the top of her field in the medical profession? An extraordinary victory. Dr. Jamison inspires me. In giving herself to the life she was given, her suffering became something positive and beneficial, not just for her own life, but for countless thousands of others.

If, like Bonnie, Scott, or Dr. Jamison, you or someone you know struggles to gain ground in the battle against bipolar disorder, congratulations. You're still in the fight. You've found the courage to live. And you've discovered strategies necessary to stay in the battle by maintaining connections with your support system, including your doctors, your family, and others within your community, and by continuing your prescribed medications. You haven't given up and allowed the siege of bipolar illness to take away your life.

But now it's time to surrender. Let go. Give in to the One who can bring you an everlasting victory. For our God is in the business of making possible the impossible. He alone will bring victory from the clutches of your defeat. "In all these things we are more than conquerors through him who loved us. For I am convinced that neither death nor life, neither angels nor demons, neither the present nor the future, nor any powers, neither height nor depth, nor anything else in all creation, will be able to separate us from the love of God that is in Christ Jesus our Lord" (Rom. 8:37–39). Amen.

EPILOGUE

Gratitude changes the pangs of memory into tranquil joy.
—Dietrich Bonhoeffer

It has been nearly two decades since I stood in Bermuda Memorial Park contemplating the best tree limb for suicide—a final act of surrender to a life-stealing adversary. Remembering sometimes hurts. It's been a long road. The seige took its toll and delivered some unavoidable seasons of suffering and waiting. But by God's grace, I surrendered to His life-giving plan and continue to emerge grateful for every part of the journey. So does Linda.

We both could choose to be bitter about the way our lives unfolded. Twelve years is a lot of "lost" time. But by receiving our past for the gift that it is, we can live with a joy-filled perspective that benefits others along their journeys. Gratitude changes everything. I heard a quote recently from Dietrich Bonhoeffer, a German theologian imprisoned and killed for his beliefs in the mid-1940s. He inspires me with this perspective: "Gratitude changes the pangs of memory into tranquil joy."

As Linda and I moved through the season following my healing in November 2002, joy did settle in, as did the desire to disperse the testimony of God's power in our lives. From that shared desire and through God's promptings, this book came to be. Eventually.

With our personal resources limited, no college degrees, and not even a typewriter, we set out on a journey toward publication, giving glory to God. Over Thanksgiving weekend in 2002, Linda wrote out an article by hand. In "My Nebuchadnezzar Experience," she presented a brief synopsis of my twelve-year battle with bipolar disorder, ending in complete physical restoration.

God showed Himself as we started talking with friends about what happened and what we wanted to do. A few thought us out of our minds. Most asked eagerly how they could help. One such individual I play tennis with and often refer to as the professor. He's retired from the city of Hopewell as their school superintendent and is super-smart.

"You don't have a typewriter?" he asked. "Well, I can type up your article in no time. Then you can submit it somewhere, like *Guideposts Magazine*." Well, I heard him right. And I did what he said I should do after he typed up the article. I submitted it to *Guideposts* with the professor cheering me on all along the way.

Within a few weeks, I received a kind letter from the editors, simply stating that my article didn't meet the magazine's criteria for publication. I wished they had suggested ideas about how to meet their criteria.

With my brainy tennis friend being so encouraging, I began to share with him my thoughts about writing a book. He didn't flinch. Instead, he engaged in the conversation and seemed genuinely interested. So I fired questions.

"How long do you think it would take me to write a book?" I asked.

He quickly replied, "About a year."

A year didn't seem like a long time to invest in an important project like a book. The possibility intrigued me. I wondered if the professor was right.

On February 17, 2003, I wrote a letter to one of Adam's friends. He worked two jobs in two different bookstores. Linda and I met him during the time Adam lived in the old farmhouse in Wake Forest, North Carolina. I hoped, based on his experience and knowledge in the book world, that he might offer suggestions for getting this book written. Unfortunately, he didn't.

Continuing our quest, I began writing letters. Lots of letters. I took advantage of every opportunity to make a contact with someone who

EPILOGUE

might help us move forward in some way. Linda and I both wanted to be obedient to what we felt God calling us to do.

In March, I began correspondence with several theologians, men whom I respected but didn't know personally. I wrote out my testimony and a letter by hand on notebook paper and sent them out to a minister in Florida. A personal reply came back within a few days offering kind words but no real advice about publishing a book. His encouragement gave me hope that we were headed down the right path and the momentum I needed to try again.

Over the coming months, I sent the same letter to three other theologians. In each case, the response indicated that the ministry existed strictly for teaching and preaching. While they appreciated my story of deliverance and thanked me for sharing it with them, none of them could recommend someone to help write our book. "Indeed, we praise God with you for your miraculous healing."

By May, I reached out in bold faith to a family-centered ministry in Colorado. To tell the truth, I didn't expect anything to come of this contact. But to leave any stone unturned seemed irresponsible. A correspondence assistant responded to my letter, not just with cordial appreciation but with helpful information. She suggested I purchase the current edition of the *Christian Writers' Market Guide* and offered the author's address and phone number for follow up.

This book contains more publishing information than I can mention in just a few lines. It lists agents, editors, magazines, publishers, and more, in addition to helpful articles on becoming a published author.

I contacted Sally Stuart right away. She graciously listened to my story over the phone. "I'm looking to hire a professional Christian writer to help write my story," I told her. She thought for a minute before recommending three different writers, providing every bit of contact information I would need.

Linda and I didn't know a thing about writing or publishing a book. We knew nothing about agents, royalties, advances, or literary contracts. Sally Stuart stands out as one of the most-sought-after speakers for Christian writers' conferences, based on her literary expertise. I was grateful for her time and commitment to helping us.

Eager to move forward with the writing of our book, I called the first name on Ms. Stuart's list and got no response. I called the second and got a recorded announcement that the number had been disconnected. With a single remaining number, I quickly dialed it and left a message with my phone number.

This author soon called back and made a strong impression on both Linda and me. She spoke of previous projects that included writing her own books as well as ghostwriting for other people. I told her my story as she listened with keen interest. "Mr. Sturt, I believe you have a worthwhile project," she assured me. Within a few days we reviewed a proposal and signed a contract for her to help us write *Bipolar Victory*.

Time came around for Linda and I to take our week at the timeshare on Virginia Beach, as we'd done each June since 1979. With greater than usual anticipation, we loaded the car and made our way. This week we would start our journey toward becoming authors. What do you think about that? Me. Ray Sturt. An author.

Once we got settled, we dove right in. Between the two of us, the story began to flow. Linda filled pages and pages of notebook paper, writing vigorously with her stash of number 2 pencils. Everywhere we went, we talked about the book. We couldn't stop talking, telling stories on top of stories. I'm surprised Linda's fingers withstood the intensity of trying to keep up!

One evening as we ate dinner, the sweetest smile grew across Linda's face. "What are you grinning about?" I asked.

"I'm feeling grateful," she said. "That's all. I guess I'm still marveling over your healing. The last several times we were here, you had some rough days. I'm always glad to be here with you, Ray. But I'm especially glad today."

My Linda. She always brings things into perspective. The truth is, I hope we'll both be marveling over my healing for the rest of our days. And that the marvel moves us to ministry. That's why we were so anxious to get our story published.

EPILOGUE

When we arrived home from the beach, Linda asked Scott for the use of his computer. He obliged, happy to help, and Linda went to his house to type up the two chapters we had been working on. Then we sent them off to our writer, who began editing and rewriting to make them suitable for an actual manuscript.

This exchange of writing dragged on for a year. In the end, much to our disappointment, only three chapters of our twelve-chapter book were completed. It became obvious to us that this relationship lacked the necessary ingredients to pull off our book project.

We acquired the services of a professional and nullified our agreement with the writer. Though we lost time and money, this allowed Linda and me to keep moving toward our goal of publication.

In late 2003, after connecting with a programming director for a major family ministry, we began sending query letters to agents. The kind-hearted young woman I spoke with advised that we seek out an agent to guide us through the writing process, as well as to promote our book properly. Based on our experiences with the writer, we knew we needed someone to represent us and *Bipolar Victory* who understood our story and our passion. Not an easy match.

Our first mailing of thirty letters went out to Christian and general-market agents and publishers early in 2004. The following year we mailed another ten letters. I had no idea how long and painful this process was going to be.

Responses to our queries varied. Some agents simply said they weren't taking on new clients. Others said they couldn't represent the subject of bipolar disorder. One agent said she had just signed a bipolar project. Another wrote "not for me" across the top and signed his name.

The president of one literary agency e-mailed saying, "The project sounds worthy." Another stated, "Very interesting." Someone else said, "Well written." One agent wrote back that her heavy work load didn't allow time at present to do the project justice. But she would keep our work on file for future consideration.

In spite of all the rejections, we kept a positive outlook. The common thread seemed to be encouragement to keep going. So we did. After all Linda and I had been through, it would take a lot to defeat us. We kept praying, asking the Lord to show us where to turn for help.

In the meantime, up through the end of 2004, we continued composing the details of our story by hand. We were already in our late fifties, and that was all we knew. A computer seemed a grand undertaking, but we asked Adam to help us consider purchasing one. He lived in North Carolina, some one hundred fifty miles from us. With an associate degree in the computer field, Adam's expertise was worth the drive. (Not to mention we love spending time with him!)

Much to our surprise, Adam suggested we keep things simple. "You just need to go buy yourselves a good electric typewriter," he said. So we did. We also bought a padded swivel office chair. Linda was set!

After studying the work of the writer we had hired, Linda figured out the basic format for the manuscript. By comparing the edited manuscript with our original one, she clued into some of the changes we needed to make going forward. And forward we went.

Linda was on a roll. She worked three days a week at the hospital, but that didn't curtail her progress on the manuscript for *Bipolar Victory*.

When our vacation weeks at the condo rolled around, we were blessed with extra time. Typically, we took three separate weeks. But in 2004–2005, we put to use each of the five weeks coming to us. Every time we made the trip out to the beach, we dragged along our typewriter, reams of paper, a good supply of ink cartridges, and all the Wite-Out we might possibly need.

I'll tell you what, those weeks were a godsend. Of course we took time off to play tennis, hit the miniature golf course, and dine at our favorite restaurants. But Linda spent hours behind the typewriter during our trips that year. We completed a whole chapter, sometimes more, each week we spent away. Linda and I truly enjoyed working

EPILOGUE

together like this. She typed and read aloud while I paced or looked over her shoulder and talked. I sometimes threw in extra tidbits just for personal flair.

As we labored through the manuscript page by page, I found myself freezing mid motion every now and again. Memories of hideous nights sent chills up my spine. Unbelievable, the way life shifted one day to the next. And there it lay, unfolding in black-and-white for all the world to see. My days of hiding in silence were definitely over.

The Lord continued to sustain the belief that our work would not be in vain. In June 2005, we received word that a publisher wanted to review our manuscript. With controlled excitement, we prepared and sent a package containing ten completed chapters, our bios, and some family photos for their consideration.

Then, with a chapter still to finish, we hit the panic button. If this publisher wanted the project, we needed to be ready. So, with Linda still working part-time at the hospital and trying to can string beans from our summer garden, we pulled together chapter 11.

A few weeks passed without a peep from the publisher. By now, we had become accustomed to riding the roller coaster of this business. You hurry up to wait. So we went on about our business.

On July 11 we received the letter we were waiting for. They wanted to publish our book! Linda and I both went facedown on the floor, thanking God for this fantastic news. Unbelievable happiness filled our house that day. Unable to keep the excitement to ourselves, we hit our circuit of family and friends with phone calls into the evening. First on the list? Adam! Our news took him by surprise. He thought we should self-publish *Bipolar Victory*. But he knew that his mom and I wanted to explore every option first. He encouraged us with his support. By the time we reached the last friend on our list, the overwhelming responses took our joy over the top.

The next few weeks happened in a flurry. At the recommendation of the publisher, we consulted with our attorney regarding their contract.

He's a professor of intellectual property law, knowledgeable and aware of fine print. His response? Don't sign.

We were shocked. He told us of other clients whose experiences with this company were less than stellar. And the contract left a lot to be desired. It padded the publisher's pockets, leaving very little for us when all was said and done. Not that Linda and I are looking for big money, but we want to be responsible with what the Lord has given.

In addition to our attorney's response, we heard other reports of unsatisfied authors who published with this company. We wanted so badly to get the word out about what God had done for us that declining this offer right away seemed crazy. So we waited. And while we waited, we continued to do what we needed to do to get the manuscript ready for publication.

This company wanted us to communicate by e-mail and to get the manuscript converted to an electronic file. We didn't have a computer, which seemed to pose a problem for them. But we were able to have the manuscript scanned at an office-supply store in Richmond. We were thrilled at the thought of getting Linda's meticulously typed pages into a usable format. But the finished file came back a jumbled up mess. Words were missing, lines were out of order. Many of the chapter headings had even disappeared. Hours and hours of work ruined.

I marched the disc right back to the store. The clerk refunded my money. It seemed a total loss. But this experience proved to be a catalyst of sorts to move us into the twenty-first century.

I went home determined. "Linda, if we're going to get this book published, we're going to need a computer."

Within the week, we were the dazed owners of a laptop. The learning curve frustrated both of us to an extreme degree. But we would not be defeated. We did our best to be patient with ourselves as we learned what we could from Adam and from our old pals, "trial and error."

Eventually I wrangled enough know-how to transfer our jumbled mess of a manuscript into a document on the computer. Then over the course of another week of vacation at the beach in 2005, we waded through the document, fixing all of the mistakes. After many hours in front of the screen, we emerged from the condo that week with our

EPILOGUE

manuscript back into sensible configuration. Finally, *Bipolar Victory* was ready for e-mailing. But we had no one to send it to.

Based on the array of negative feedback from professionals in the field, we turned down the publisher's offer. Some thought us crazy to turn down a "live" contract. But we didn't sense God giving us a green light. He seemed, instead, to be asking us to wait. Again. Perhaps still.

Seasons of waiting can be excruciating, even for us "pros." We did our best to stay focused on the future, trust in God's timing, and to do what we could to make ourselves ready for opportunities when they came. But after sending out another twenty agent queries without much response, our energy started to wane. Linda became especially frustrated and wanted to walk away from the book and anything associated with bipolar.

We tried one more time to connect with a well-known pastor from the West Coast. He boasted in a television interview that he had helped another person find a writer and an agent. That's all we wanted. To hear back from him at all would have gone a long way to restoring our faith that we should continue our quest. But nothing.

Discouragement set in. Not so much for me, but for my lovely wife. Linda was done. We understood waiting and believed very much in God's sovereign will. But 2005 rolled into 2006 without much encouragement. Something had to give. And give it did.

When Linda showed up for the January meeting of her Christian Women's Club, she met with a surprise. The keynote speaker stood and recounted the story of her son's battle with bipolar disorder. Though he professed faith in Christ, he turned to drugs to help alleviate his pain. "No one knows the constant agony I struggle with every single day," he told his mom. "The voices in my head never go away." The drugs eventually landed him in prison. He died his first day there from cocaine poisoning.

God spoke to Linda in a profound way through this woman's testimony. She came home with renewed vigor, ready to receive the ministry God had for her, for us. "Ray, we have to move forward with *Bipolar Victory*. We just have to."

Letting God lead isn't always easy. But it is always right. We found courage through Him to write our story. Now we needed courage to continue living His story. Trusting Him to show us His way, in His timing. Being obedient to wait until He says go. Responding to the opportunities He brings when He brings them.

In one of our favorite devotionals, *Morning and Evening,* Charles H. Spurgeon encouraged us with these words: "'Stand firm'—keep the posture of an upright man, ready for action, expecting further orders, cheerfully and patiently awaiting the directing voice; and it will not be long before God shall say to you, as directly as Moses said it to the people of Israel, 'Go forward.'"

But God didn't release the Israelites to "go" until after they journeyed through the wilderness. The long route. Forty years of wandering. Forty years of life-giving miracles and opportunities to know and love the God who set them free.

So we waited. And we journeyed. And we lived.

With Linda's fibromyalgia worsening, we decided to downsize our lives by selling our tri-level home. We loved our big garden, the pool, and the spa. But the amount of time and care everything required began to overwhelm us. Going up and down the two flights of stairs wore Linda out. They were even too much for our aging Sophie. We needed a simpler lifestyle.

And God provided one. In Hopewell! We purchased a small lot in an age-qualified community. Beautiful mature trees and a bubbling creek bordered our property. We couldn't believe it! We could make a new home together in this parklike setting, and Sophie would love trailing around, sniffing out our new neighborhood.

The week of Christmas 2006, we watched as a construction crew poured the foundation of our new brick home. Throughout the spring, our excitement grew, brick by brick. And on May 15, 2007, we officially

EPILOGUE

moved into the place where we would celebrate the beginning of a new season.

We left our old home, thankful for the sweet memories of raising our boys there, as well as for the memories, lessons, and miracles that came out of the enemy's seige. We acknowledged each as a valuable part in our journey.

Every day brought movement and assurance in the sovereignty of our God. Even through the rolling hills of anticipation and disappointment, we found in Him strength to continue seeking help to publish our book, as He provided opportunity. One agent in Florida requested a review of *Bipolar Victory,* not on disc or by e-mail, but by snail mail. What do you think about that? She wanted a neat, typewritten copy of the full manuscript. We obliged her request, and she offered a contract for her representation services. But once more, our consulting attorney advised against the arrangement. We were getting good at waiting.

And we were getting good at letting God care for our needs, leading us down His path, not our own. In September, four months after our move, He provided a lovely Christian family to purchase our thirty-three-year-old home. Though the market was down, we hadn't contacted a realtor. We simply put a sign in the yard and began to pray, trusting that God would fulfill His plan for our old home in His time. What a great God He is!

When October came, Linda turned sixty-two. With her health taking a toll and the blessing of our refreshed circumstances, she decided to retire from her nursing position at John Randolph Medical Center. After serving patients faithfully throughout her thirty-nine-year career, not to mention the demanding "patient" she had had under her own roof for twelve years, Linda deserved a break.

She got her break and then some! Within a few months, God slowed her down even further as her health declined. In January 2008, doctors concluded that her gallbladder needed to come out.

As happens so often when we're paying attention, this unexpected rest turned out to be perfect timing for gathering loose ends on our project. While recovering from surgery, Linda began to pour over every word of *Bipolar Victory*. From chapter 1 right on through to the end, she corrected errors and edited out phrases that didn't belong. She polished and revised for weeks, preparing for the day of publication that we believed would come.

I admit, waiting sometimes wore us thin. Maybe the snares we encountered in the five years since our publication journey began were small compared to the ones we endured while under seige. In the middle of it all, the enemy really poked at us, filling us with doubt and insecurities. Maybe we hadn't heard God. Maybe this couldn't be done. Who were we to think that we might have something to encourage others who suffer through the life-threatening horrors of a bipolar seige? And hope? It was fading. Fast.

But we serve a God whose ways are not our own. He's always at work. And His timing is always right.

In 2008, we risked entering the real estate market again. Scott had been renting an older home from us for years, but he really needed something closer to his job. In no time at all, we found a like-new ranch-style home just a mile away from the Lowe's where Scott worked. His move motivated us to sell the house in spite of the continuing economic crisis. So we took out the same "For Sale by Owner" sign we had used the summer before to sell our tri-level and stuck it smack in the middle of the front yard. Then we prayed. And we waited.

Nine months later, a man came along who needed a home in the area. Once again, God was at work. In His timing and in His way, He provided. We were so blessed.

With the sale of our homes, and by making some changes with other investments, we began to see God remove the obstacle of finances from our path to publication. He also began to open our eyes once again to the possibility of publishing Bipolar Victory ourselves. In spite of all the snags, we knew that we were to somehow get our story out there. And God seemed to be providing a way for His life-giving message of hope to be put into the hands of those suffering under seige.

EPILOGUE

So we followed His command to "Go forward."

After years of wandering and waiting, we contacted the WinePress Publishing Group in the spring of 2009. Washington State seemed a long ways away, but the company came highly recommended. I spoke with their representatives, and we reviewed their brochures, all the while praying for wisdom. In April we signed a contract and began the next season of our journey—a season not without snags of its own.

After several months went by, WinePress informed us of a big snag. A snag that stung and would cost us much more money than a simple edit of the original manuscript. They recommended that we work with a professional writer to more effectively bring out the heart of our story.

Bipolar Victory—the living and the telling of it—was a journey of faith long before we breathed a breath about publishing a book. We looked to the Lord for His guidance, and His answer came back the same. "Go forward." We only had one response: "Yes!"

In January 2010, Robin Stanley agreed to come alongside us to tell our story. She fought side by side with us in the battle of bringing our message to print, surrendering with us, time and again, to the will of our sovereign God. Together, we labored in pursuit of *Bipolar Victory*, not for our own sake, but for the purpose and glory of God our Father. Amen.

Now, it's your turn to "go forward." Find victory by surrendering your life to the Lord who gave it.

NOTES

1. "About Mood Disorders," Depression and Bipolar Support Alliance, http://www.dbsalliance.org/site/PageServer?pagename=about_MDOverview (accessed April 13, 2011).
2. Carrie Fisher interview by Diane Sawyer, *Primetime,* ABC, December 21, 2000.
3. "George Muller," GoodReads, http://www.goodreads.com/author/quotes/199772.George_Muller (accessed April 15, 2011).
4. Dr. Kay Redfield Jamison, "The Benefits of Restlessness and Jagged Edges," *The Saturday Evening Post,* September/October 2005.

WinePressPublishing
Great Books, Defined.

To order additional copies of this book call:
1-877-421-READ (7323)
or please visit our website at
www.WinePressbooks.com

If you enjoyed this quality custom-published book,
drop by our website for more books and information.

www.winepresspublishing.com
"Your partner in custom publishing."